Jest For Fun

Lois A. Corcoran

Hard Shell Word Factory

Trade paperback
ISBN-13: 978-0-7599-4782-5
ISBN-10: 0-7599-4782-1
Published January 2007

© 2005 Lois Corcoran
eBook ISBN: 0-7599-4781-3
Published April 2005

Hard Shell Word Factory
PO Box 161
Amherst Jct. WI 54407
books@hardshell.com
www.hardshell.com
Cover art © 2005 Dirk A. Wolf

Table of Contents

CHAPTER ONE - CLEANING UP MY ACT

A COMPLIMENTARY COLUMN

MARK TWAIN IS said to have quipped, "I can live for two months on a good compliment." So I watched how folks reacted to praise at an awards ceremony I attended a while back. The honorees displayed no embarrassment whatsoever as the emcee raved *ad nauseam* about their many achievements. And in their acceptance speeches, not one of them said, "Aw, shucks...it was nothin'."

Personally, I have trouble accepting compliments and there is a physiological explanation for this. The blood that normally flows to my brain is rerouted to make my cheeks blush. Hence, the exchange goes something like this:

Praiser: That outfit looks really nice on you.

Me: What are ya, nuts? The hem is falling down and look at this stain! I've tried *everything* to get it out...

According to a French guy named Francois de Le Something-Or-Other, "When we disclaim praise, it is only showing our desire to be praised a second time." *Au contraire*, François. Once is *more* than enough to throw me into a dither.

Either that or I enter my Analysis Mode. I'm the only one I know of who can get defensive over compliments (i.e., "What do you *mean* by that?"). Or I'll ponder the praiser's motivation. Is this a sincere compliment? I ask myself. And, if not, what does this doofus hope to gain by flattering me?

I could tell that none of the award recipients entertained unsavory thoughts like that. Instead, they strode up confidently to receive their honors and spewed out well-rehearsed acceptance speeches. Like Academy Award winners, they thanked every Tom, Dick and Harriet who ever crossed their path. And they shared more than we needed to know about their life histories.

While I admired their self-assurance, it occurred to me there might be a better way to show their gratitude. Surely there exists a happy medium between their method and mine. So I did a little research to learn what should have been taught in kindergarten: The best way to accept praise is to smile, look the person straight in the eyes and say "Thank you." Nothing more and nothing less.

So I practiced in the mirror and have been all set to field a compliment for some time now. Trouble is, I haven't gotten any lately. I'll bet it's been at *least* two months.

Yoohoo! I'm over here!

CLEANING UP MY ACT

I VOWED I WOULD NEVER surf the Net for that sort of thing. Normally it's not my idea of entertainment, but curiosity got the best of me. With an innocent click of the mouse, I got an eyeful at The Web Site for People Who Love to Clean (howtocleanit.com).

Given my iffy housekeeping, I felt a little out of my element. It was nevertheless a friendly site, with smiling maids and helpful tips. Reminded me of my mom. She springcleans whether it's spring or not. Her clean gene also found its way to my sister, June Cleaver. Given this strong family trait, I'm reasonably certain I'm adopted.

Maybe I'm just sensitive, but I've noticed more infomercials about cleaning lately. One demonstrated a super-duper vacuum that blazed a trail through someone's spotless looking bed-and-breakfast. I hoped they would dump soil on the rug, but instead they removed debris already there, much to the innkeeper's over-dramatized embarrassment. Like, get over it! My vacuum could learn a lot from that show, though. It wouldn't detect dirt if I rubbed its nose in it.

With feet propped up and working my way through some popcorn, I sat through an equally compelling advertisement for the Steam Buggy. "Do you need a gas mask to clean your commode?" the announcer asked. He must have peeked.

Moments later, a female grime fighter landed on the scene, armed with the peculiar device. She showed us viewers how to rid ourselves of grease, soap scum, mold, mildew and other dirty words. To say nothing of money. Then she flew off with a big S on her cape.

As if that wasn't a big enough hint, I got this catalog in the mail the other day from a speed cleaning company. It offered products and sanitizing advice for everything, *including* the kitchen sink. As I browsed through some foreign-looking scrubbing supplies I thought, *Are you people trying to tell me something?* Right then and there I made a life-changing decision.

So I plan to invite the vacuum cleaner guy, the Steam Buggy lady, and the catalog experts here this week. In the comfort of my home they can demonstrate their products to their little hearts' content.

And while they clean and disinfect the place, I'm gonna search the Web for my birth family.

CIA (CORKY'S INVESTIGATION AGENCY)

"LOOKS LIKE THE Joneses are having pizza for supper," I announced after spotting a familiar delivery car. I may not be the sharpest hook in the tackle box, but I know a sure sign when I see one. Although I pondered which toppings were ordered, I stifled the urge to call and probe.

One of the great perks of small town living is the opportunity to snoop on neighbors. My favorite character on *Bewitched* had to be Gladys Kravitz, the nosy lady who witnessed all sorts of strange goings-on. With binoculars in hand, she'd shriek over these incidents to her disinterested husband, Abner, and nag him to take a look.

Actress Sandra Gould may have died, but her Gladys role is alive and well. People are bound to be curious about the folks they rub picket fences with. Just for the record, I want to assure any neighbors reading this that I don't resort to binoculars. Not when my telescope works so well. Even better, the naked eye is more readily available and requires fewer adjustments.

Of course, snooping is a two-way street. While I theorize on what's happening at the Jones', it's likely the Smiths are raising eyebrows over *my* habits. A few years back, a handsome young man paid a call to take my picture for the local paper. After inviting him in, I promptly closed the drapes. Later, I fell all over myself explaining it to a neighbor. I just didn't want the photo overexposed, okay, Gen?

There's a world of difference between innocent snooping and out-and-out spying. Despite my natural curiosity, I wouldn't *consider* installing a video camera. It shocked me to learn nearly two-thirds of the country's employers use tactics like that to spy on the hired help. Other methods include recording phone calls and reading email. And it's perfectly legal!

I'm fiercely opposed to this type of sneaky activity. Workers deserve more respect than that. How can they give themselves a decent manicure when they're being scrutinized this way? Instead, business owners who want to keep tabs should work alongside their employees. They'd learn all they need to know and then some.

Now if you'll excuse me, I need to go find out—er—help a neighbor of mine...

DON'T PLAY IT AGAIN, SAM

WE'VE ALL HEARD that music hath charms to soothe the savage breast, but sometimes it "hath" the opposite effect.

Take, for instance, the true story of a lighthouse keeper at Seguin Island, Maine. When he bought his lonely wife a piano, she faithfully practiced the only sheet of music she possessed and soon played it with fervor. Day after day she pounded the keys 'til it finally drove the keeper insane. One night he hacked up the piano before turning the axe on his wife. Too bad she couldn't ad lib—a little *Chopsticks* to break the monotony perhaps.

I can't picture that happening here because I rarely play our old upright. It's desperately out of tune and the keys have a tendency to stick. This means plucking them up manually if I hope to finish a song.

Despite its enormous bulk, I often forget it's there. In fact, our cat tickles the ivories more than I do. Heard her jump on them the other day and she didn't sound half bad. Unlike her, I play by ear and that organ gets a little forgetful at times.

For a change of pace, I like to haul out my keyboard, although its narrow keys make fingering a bit of a challenge. When I get tired of the inevitable mistakes, I press a button and it plays a perfect tune all by itself. It occurs to me all instruments should come equipped with that feature. Singers, too, for that matter.

My brother recently developed an interest in the guitar. I requested a concert after he'd had a few lessons and listened to an accurate though painstaking rendition of *Tom Dooley*.

"Bravo!" I hollered over my applause. "Now play *Classical Gas*!"

That's an old favorite of mine, although just listening to it tires me out these days. Mason Williams must take Geritol before a performance.

To steal an old joke, I bought a tin whistle the other day and now I tin whistle. As a quality instrument, it ranks somewhere between a tonette and a kazoo. On the plus side, it takes no time at all to learn, unlike the clarinet I spent years squawking on, only to forget the basics.

Maybe some day I'll gather all my instruments and arrange a recital. Sort of a one-woman-band kind of thing.

But first I'd better hide my husband's axe.

FEAR OF SPUBLIC PEAKING

OUT OF THE blue, I got a call from Emily, an old friend and award-winning poet, who asked if I'd teach a workshop on humor writing. As one who prefers my padded, little comfort zone, I ummed and ahhed my way through some feeble excuses.

"We'll pay you fifty bucks," Emily said brightly.

And before I could stifle it, my tongue betrayed me.

Thus I spent the next week in a state of high anxiety. In the name of research, I scanned dozens of books for samples of knee-slappers. Then I worked them into a highly entertaining speech. Or so I thought.

My first audience consisted of eight-year-old son, Kelly, who yawned loudly two minutes into the presentation. Later my husband, Dan, showed similar enthusiasm.

"Maybe it's my delivery," I mumbled to myself, and wondered if there's a workshop for teaching people how to teach a workshop. Finding none, I studied Dale Carnegie's guide, *How to Develop Self-Confidence and Influence People by Public Speaking*. His books are well known for their positive themes, common sense and Steve-Austin-size titles.

In a nutshell, I learned I must force myself to act brave while at the podium. Never mind my right eye twitches and my voice smacks of helium abuse.

Kelly, by strange coincidence, gave his own talk the day before mine and offered some wisdom. "Just pretend you're talking to yourself in a mirror, Mom." Seeing as I do that on a regular basis, I found his advice easier to follow.

Fifty-some revisions and a ream of paper later, the big day arrived, and with it, inclement weather. *Surely they'll call the conference off,* I thought…but no. Shedding my parka and clenching the speech in my tight, little fist, I made my entrance and looked around.

The audience wasn't much bigger than when I'd practiced in the mirror. Not counting us speakers, a grand total of six showed up. Still, I felt a rush of jitters.

"My name is Lois Corcoran," I began, "and I have a fear of spublic peaking." Their polite chuckle helped me relax. Not to the point of reclining, maybe, but enough to deliver my address, which was met with equally polite applause. *Gee, that wasn't so bad,* I thought afterward.

And when I stepped back into my comfort zone, it seemed a little less confining.

A FEW CHOICE WORDS

WHILE AGONIZING OVER what to write about this week, it occurred to me I have trouble making decisions. The other day I spent twenty-odd minutes deciding what to wear. I discarded mountains of clothes 'til I found something suitable that, by strange coincidence, happened to fit. Then I pulled on my coat and went grocery shopping.

By the way, that is the worst (just so the sentence structure isn't identical to that above) thing a choice-challenged person can do. I mean, have you any idea how many brands of breakfast cereal exist? An entire aisle is devoted to food we eat while still unconscious.

Toothpaste is just as bad. After skimming the hurdle of which brand to buy, I'm left to ponder over regular, tartar control or baking soda. The lights dim and dramatic music plays as I consider the options. After a tense, sweat-inducing moment, I yell, "Cool mint gel! Final answer!" Applause rings in my ears as I steer my cart up the next aisle.

And decisions don't end at the supermarket. The gas station offers multiple choices, too, like unleaded, super unleaded and premium unleaded. C'mon, folks! What exactly is the difference? Gas is gas, isn't it? After making a selection, I must decide how to pay—with cash, check or body parts.

But the ultimate challenge for people like me is the World Wide Web. No matter what site I visit, it offers links to dozens—make that hundreds—of companion pages and like-minded sites. And vying for my undivided attention, assorted ad buttons compete with each other by flashing or hopping around on the screen. "Click here!" they shout. "No, click *here!*"

Ironically, I've had no problem making huge, life-altering decisions such as whether to marry or where to work. The prospects presented themselves and it was like, "Hey, go for it!" What bogs me down are those nitpicky dilemmas that creep up more often than my underwear...

...which brings me back to the clothing conundrum. But I'm not alone. Check out the marital closet in *any* home and you'll see women's clothes far outnumber men's. To aid us in this and other areas, there's a book called *Simplify Your Life* (Elaine St. James). This nifty little paperback suggests, among other things, that we "build a simple wardrobe."

So I took that advice and tossed out everything in my closet. And next time you see me I'll be in uniform.

GAINLESSLY EMPLOYED

I'LL NEVER FORGET a colorful co-worker I used to have. Rarely at a loss for words, she nevertheless had little to say when she was terminated. But her actions spoke volumes when she dropped her drawers and mooned the office on her way out.

I may be retired, but I still recall the ups and downs of employment and the burden of finding it in the first place. I'd spend hours updating a resumé to reflect my vast knowledge and experience. The job where I did naught but answer the phone, for example, translated to "excellent communica-tion skills." Even more impressive, I once typed a fifty-page brief without getting nail polish on the keyboard.

But as a rule, my knock-'em-dead resumé fell on blind eyes which, frankly, was a big relief. Winning an interview gave me a bad case of the jitters. I'd have to wipe my sweaty palms on my career girl outfit before shaking hands with the Head Honcho. Then my heart thumped like a jackhammer and I'd babble in this extra-terrestrial voice.

Still, I landed over a dozen jobs before becoming a columnist. Trouble is, being gainlessly employed as a writer is like perpetually seeking employment. Instead of a resumé, I send out samples, secure in the knowledge they'll line someone's trash bin. If it weren't for rejections, I'd get no reply at all.

Every leap year or so, I luck out but, there again, my paranoia works overtime. What if they don't like my stuff? Worse yet, what if I can't think of something new to write? Facing an ongoing deadline is like having to draft a term paper every week. And fretting that I'll flunk.

Often my brain suffers from constipation. I sit down all prepared, but not a trace comes out. Even Ex-Lax doesn't help.

But I never give up because, as a former boss of mine likes to remind me, a writer writes. And when at last I succeed, I savor the feeling of accomplishment for all of five minutes before fussing over what to write next.

Hardest of all is when a newspaper drops my column. My brain understands budget cuts, but all my ego hears is "You stink!" As discouraging as that is, I try to accept the decision with grace and dignity.

Right after I pull up my drawers.

GETTING THAT (THIRD) DEGREE

WHILE YAKKING ON the phone the other day, a friend and I turned our discussion to higher education. "You have your four-year, don't you?" she asked.

"Well, ah...not quite," I stammered.

"Associate?"

"Er, um...not that either," I said.

"You mean you never went to college?"

"Bingo!" I squeaked.

In a world obsessed with the almighty diploma, it's tough admitting I lack one. Sure, I graduated from high school. But I spent my late teens wondering what I wanted to be when I grew up and, frankly, I'm still in the dark.

I would've made a classic career student though. Using my home-decorating tactics—On second thought, the couch looks better over there—I'd change my major every few months and acquired the student loan debts to prove it.

How do people know which vocation best suits them until they've actually tried it? I know countless individuals who, upon obtaining a degree, settled into a job they grew to loathe. And a fair number of graduates find employment in totally unrelated fields.

There are plenty of exceptions, of course. For those who know where they're going in life, college opens the door to the Golden Goose. The son of a pal of mine likes computers. He went to college for computers. And now he needs a computer to tally his obscene income.

So I'm all for higher education. I just never felt compelled to get that (third) degree. Until now.

Checking my email this morning, I saw an ad for "Diplomas based on your present knowledge and life experience..." Heck, I've got *loads* of experience so I read on. "...Bachelors, masters and doctorate diplomas available in the field of your choice..." Personally, I'd opt for the PhD. "...No one is turned down." *Not even me?*

So I dialed the number faster than you can say telephone scam. The nice young man who answered told me my highly credible degree can arrive by courier in less than ten business days. The fee? Sixteen hundred bucks.

"Isn't that a little steep for a piece of paper?" I asked.

"Most of that goes for support," he explained.

"Could you expand on that?"

"When you sign up," he continued, "I'll tell you more about our Backup Aid for Investigated Licensees."

"Don't tell me—BAIL for short, right? Well...hey, thanks for the info. I've gotta run..."

"Wait!" he cried, "I didn't get your credit card number!"
Click.

ITCHING TO LOSE WEIGHT

I'VE SPENT HALF my lifetime trying to lose weight. The last product I tried took the form of a magic elixir made from sixteen mysterious plants.

"It's possible to lose eight to ten pounds per week!" the two-page ad claimed, so I waited anxiously for my vials to arrive. Like a mad scientist, I squeezed out the recommended dosage into a glass of water and guzzled it before each meal.

Half expecting to grow fur, I glanced in the bathroom mirror the next day, but my mug looked the same. Unfortunately, the scale didn't change either. "What the heck?" I said aloud, scratching my head. My back itched, so I scratched that, too. In fact, I clawed every *inch* of me. But the gnarly red welts that appeared were the real tip-off.

Hmmm, I thought. *I must be allergic to this stuff.* So I mailed the potion back with a polite letter requesting a refund or I'd sue their association. They promptly granted my request.

While magazine ads are fairly convincing, nothing promotes the diet industry like TV. Each morning on the Weather Channel, I suffer through the same commercial for pills that allegedly block fat. It shows this aerobic queen eating cake in her bikini—as though normal people do that. Then again, she looks like she's a few reps short of a set.

Speaking of exercise, television zealously sells all manner of muscle toning equipment. I sat through an ad the other day for an odometer and heard the announcer spaz out over its many features.

"Now you can have more fun than ever jogging!" he gushed.

Like, is he serious? The 'amazing' device keeps track of how far you've run or walked and how many steps you've taken. In addition, it plays various tunes with really poor acoustics. But wait—there's more! It also offers an alarm—a handy feature if you routinely fall asleep jogging.

For once, I held onto my purse and chose to live without the fat-blocking pills and the handy dandy odometer. Instead I plan to use good old-fashioned common sense.

I wonder where I can buy some.

THE JOY OF ENTREPRENEURSHIP?

I FELT A DEEP NEED to teach my eight-year-old the Joy of Entrepreneurship. "With a little hard work," I said, planting a hand firmly on his shoulder, "anything can succeed." A few corny clichés like that convinced Kelly to help prepare for the annual rummage sale. Or was it to shut me up?

For weeks we gathered idle belongings 'til finally the big day arrived. You may recall that previous sales were sabotaged by rain, wind and other circumstances beyond my control. But this year the sun smiled down on us. Or was that a sneer?

Early that morning, I carted our merchandise up the basement stairs and out to the yard. What I thought would take thirty minutes devoured two beastly hours. Finally, we anchored signs around town and returned to our store. Having worked up a healthy sweat, I wrung myself out and sat down to wait for customers.

Strangely enough, things started out with a lull. It took half an hour for someone to wander over. She eyed up several big-ticket items before buying a toy for twenty-five cents.

"See?" I told Kelly. "All we needed was a little patience." Thus began a lecture on perseverance. When I finished yakking, I realized another lull had settled—even longer than the first. And another. And another.

"I can't believe it, Kell," I griped. "After all our hard work, nobody's coming!"

"Maybe they're eating lunch, Mom," Kelly said.

"For three hours?"

Sometime during what I loosely term a sale, the sky turned gray. "I think it's gonna rain, Mom," Kelly warned.

"No, those are just cumulous clouds," I said, sliding in a science lesson. "Besides, it feels kinda good to have some shade."

An hour and fifteen cents later, I admitted defeat. We made the rounds to retrieve our signs and got back in time for the downpour. I scooted around like a cockroach, snatching up items I'd taken great pains to display earlier. After a hundred trips to the basement, I slumped into a chair.

And there I pouted until remembering that one remaining task—counting the money. With my last shred of energy, I handed the cash box to Kelly. He carefully stacked the coins in neat little rows before announcing the verdict. "Hey, Mom! We made $6.35!"

"Like I said before, kiddo—with a little hard work, anything can succeed."

Or is that suck?

JUST TEETHING

LAST TIME I WROTE a column about it, a member of the dental profession drilled me a new orifice. (Geez, lady, I was just teething!) So today I vow to give the subject the utmost respect. After all, the *last* person I wanna provoke is a dentist.

It all started when I ate a Fudgesicle™ the other day. The cold confection touched a sensitive tooth and I shot clear into Canada. When I awoke at two the next morning, my mouth throbbed and the day went downhill from there.

I'd best make an appointment, I thought with mounting anxiety and picked up the phone. "Is it true he's good with kids?" I asked the receptionist.

"Uh-huh," she replied.

"Good, 'cause I'm a big baby."

A cancellation had left a cavity in her appointment book, so she penciled me in. Knowing I'd be in no condition to dine afterward, I fixed myself The Last Supper, brushed my teeth and headed out the door. I strode off with false courage until a neighbor revved up his circular saw.

As a new patient, I completed a two-page form, which, among other things, requested my next of kin. My hand shook as I signed at the bottom.

Soon a Vanna White-type assistant draped me with an apron heavier than my caramel rolls. After my teeth were x-rayed, the dentist made his entrance. Young and professional, he was the last word in thorough. Handsome, too, and I tried to spit as suavely as possible.

He analyzed the x-rays and examined my cracked tooth before recommending a crown. A veteran bargain hunter, I opted for a filling instead and, soon, the anesthetic took effect.

"Duzh everyone who worksh in a dental offish have a perfect shmile?" I flirted between drillings.

He said he once had an assistant with teeth missing, but she didn't last long.

I watched in fascination as instruments of all shapes and sizes visited my gaping mouth, which, by now, was fine with the whole thing. The dentist probed it with an explorer, which is not a car, (although there was room) but a glorified nut pick. And, before long, my tooth was happy again.

It suffered a setback when the lidocaine wore off, but I rubbed some whiskey on it, save for the portion that trickled down my throat. And I toasted the members of the dental profession.

LOOKING FOR MR. CLEAN

ONE OF MY duties as a mean, old mother is to instill healthy habits in my eight-year-old. Each day I send him to the bathroom before mealtime, and each day he emerges with the dirt still firmly in place.

"I asked you to wash your hands," I told him one day.

"I *did!*" he replied.

"Then how come the soap is still dry?" I asked after a personal investigation.

The next time I found it in need of CPR, but Kelly miraculously stayed dirty. When I questioned him, my Number One Son informed me, "If the soap is wet, it means I washed my hands."

"If the soap is wet, it means you wet the soap," I argued.

One day he asked, "Why do I have to wash my hands if I use a fork?"

I seized the opportunity to lecture about personal cleanliness and good health. Apparently, I was somewhat convincing because, when Kelly exited the head, his right paw looked fairly decent. By way of explanation, he said, "I'm only gonna eat with this hand."

To his credit, I've seen some improvement. It's a tad easier reading his palms these days. But the cleaner he gets his hands, the grimier he leaves the sink, to say nothing of my bath towels. I'd hate to see a finger bowl when he finished with it. Furthermore, if he takes longer than five minutes, I have to wade through a foot of water to retrieve him.

As with anything else, there's a right way and a wrong way to wash hands. The proper method involves scrubbing both sides of your hands for roughly thirty seconds. Great. But what about the faucets in restrooms that shut off when you let go of the handle? Should we operate them with our tootsies? And after all that diligent sanitizing, who wants to touch a public bathroom door handle laden with cooties?

According to an article I read, hands should be washed:

1. After using the john
2. After blowing your nose
3. Before fixing or eating food
4. After touching raw meat.

I can think of a few colorful activities to add to that list, but will leave them to your imagination.

At any rate, now that Kelly's better about cleaning up before meals, I'll work on those other hand washing moments. But one thing's for sure—he'll never be a surgeon.

MEET ME IN ST. LOIS?

THANKS TO ONE of my savvy readers, I heard about an elite club that has my name written all over it. Founded in 1979, it's called the Lois Club and its members are all named—I'll give you three guesses—Lois.

The lady who called me hopes to get a local chapter started. I'm not sure how she feels about her moniker, but I have a problem with mine. Maybe it was the Superman joke I heard all my life. ("Hey, Lois— Where's Clark Kent?") How terribly original.

Or perhaps it was because otherwise intelligent folks had a tendency to slaughter its pronunciation. I've shuddered over Lewis, Louise, Luey and—how shall I word this?—Low-Arse. Small wonder I'm not crazy about the name.

It's not a real common handle either. I can count on one hand the number of Loises I know and wondered from time to time about the ones I don't. Are they young or old, rich or poor, fat or thin? And how do they feel about *their* name?

So I searched the Web for information on the Lois Club. Turns out the idea originated in Minnesota when Lois Millner bought life insurance from Lois Weston and they went out to lunch. Thanks to newspaper and TV exposure, the Lois Club grew and chapters sprouted up in other states. It even seeped across the border where there are over fifteen hundred Canadian members. Gosh, whodathunk?

These aren't just mild-mannered ladies who eat Lois Lunches— they've even gone down under. No, not under the table—under the planet. While there, they strolled down (what else but?) Lois Lane. They even gazed out over Lois Lake, named after little Lois Aitken. As the story goes, a rope and chair were rigged up to cross the lake, and Lois's brothers would send her halfway across and leave her hanging there. Where's Superman when you need him?

Hard telling. But a statue of the action figure resides in Metropolis, Illinois, and guess which sisterhood paid a visit.

The Lois Club has also toured Ireland and Germany and taken cruises all over tarnation. And everywhere they go, they recruit more

Loises. There are fifty-six members in New Zealand, of all places. Man—we're, like, taking over the world!

If *you* want a piece of the action, please email tovarlois@hotmail.com. And tell her Lois sent ya.

A MODERN INCONVENIENCE

DID YOU HEAR about the dog who ate a cell phone? Don't look for a punch line. It really happened that Charlie, an indiscriminating bloodhound, gulped down the device without his master's knowledge. When Londoner Rachel Murray dialed her cell phone number, the pooch's stomach rang.

The next day Charlie—er—dumped the evidence. Just for the record, the phone still works, but I, for one, would hesitate to use it.

We Corcorans should be so lucky as to have our phone swallowed. I find that modern convenience pretty inconvenient. Almost without exception, the party on the other end wants something from me.

"Can we count on you for a donation to Save the What's-its?"

Or, "Could you bake a pan of bars for such-and-such?"

Just once I'd like someone to call and say, "We wanna bake *you* a pan of bars!"

Friends and family aren't immune from the telephonic gimme's either, i.e., "Junior's selling toothbrushes for Cub Scouts. Can we sign you up for a dozen?"

But the requests most likely to grind my teeth start out, "You don't have a job so would you mind..."

Our family doesn't believe in plastic money, but that doesn't stop credit card companies from trying their darnedest to recruit us. "You'll pay no annual fee (but lots of monthly ones!) with an Acme Credit Card." Telemarketers are trained not to breathe until they've finished their spiel, and I've heard shorter presidential debates.

I've gone beyond screening my calls. It's to the point I'd like to yank our modern convenience off the kitchen wall. But I recently read about a less violent solution. An enterprising attorney named Kenneth Jursinski invented the Phone Butler. Whatever the situation, irritated consumers need only press a button to activate the device. Callers are promptly transferred to a distinguished voice with a proper British accent:

"Pardon me. This is the Phone Butler, and I have been directed to inform you that this household must respectfully decline your inquiry. Kindly place this number on your do-not-call list. Good day."

What a classy solution! Sure, it's kind of pricey, but think of the money you'll save in valium prescriptions. To thwart unwanted callers, order your Phone Butler at www.phonebutler.com.

Or find yourself a good bloodhound.

A MONKEY ON MY BACK

IT STARTED IN high school. I thought it looked cool when other kids did it, so I tried it myself. Now a quarter century later, I still have a monkey on my back. Or at least it looks that way from twenty-five years of slouching.

Some days you'd swear my spine was surgically removed. I should have gone to finishing school where students practiced good posture by walking with a book on their heads. But with my luck, I'd have gotten an encyclopedia.

Being a secretary for two decades didn't help matters. Shoulders tend to slouch from parking in front of a computer all day—except in times of high stress. On those occasions, they defied gravity. While I pounded out some crucial document, my shoulders mysteriously rose to ear level, giving me that Schroeder-at-the-piano appearance.

When this strange phenomenon happens, experts recommend three exercises for relief:

1. Rotate your head slowly from side to side.
2. Try circling your arms like a windmill without collapsing your cubicle walls.
3. Kick off those high heels (or wingtips) and stretch your body fully to the left and right. (This also works as a turn signal on the way to the coffee room.)

Helpful, yes. But what happens when the boss stops by to see the Smith contract while you're imitating Jane Fonda?

The answer may lie in hiring a personal drill sergeant—someone who follows you throughout the day barking, "Stomach in! Chest out!"

"It *is* out!" I'd squeak defensively.

Mail order catalogs offer a calmer solution to poor posture. The upper body brace aligns the spine and pulls back the shoulders, forcing the dejected girl in the "before" picture to stand up and take notice.

Aside from the device looking a bit restrictive, I wondered about those dozen magnets inside. True, they've proven helpful in the field of medicine, but they could wreak havoc on my computer system. And what happens if I, wearing my lovely magnetic brace, become hopelessly attached to my file cabinet?

No. To break a habit, one must simply be conscious of it. Writing this column required me to think about posture all week. Now that I'm done, I'll stay focused by typing, I will not slouch a hundred times a day.

Now where's that copy-and-paste key again?

MUSINGS FROM BILL GATES' MOTHER

"I PRACTICE SAFE COMPUTING," my eight-year-old son joked one day.

"Excuse me?" I said, casting a sidelong glance in his direction.

"I read that in *The Complete Idiot's Guide*," Kelly explained.

He studies one called, *Creating HTML Web Pages* in bed darn near every night. Though it would effectively lull *me* to sleep, it only serves to kindle his interest in PCs. Last year I caught him reading *The Computer Users' Dictionary*, a book filled with geeky terms and their meanings.

"Where did I go wrong?" I asked, shaking my head.

Some days, I swear I gave birth to Bill Gates. When Kelly isn't computing or *reading* about computing, he's sliding computer lingo into normal conversation. The other day, for instance, we looked everywhere for a lost mitten without success. Returning home he announced, "The search is complete. There are no results to display."

Like his mother, Kelly would prefer to have summer last nine months and the other seasons a month each. "I wish we could restart the year with new settings," he told me once.

Then there was the time we discussed the Gettysburg Address and how, contrary to popular belief, President Lincoln made numerous revisions to the famous speech. "Too bad he didn't have MS Word to make it easier," Kelly observed.

"Ya," I agreed. "Poor guy probably had one of those old DOS programs, hey?"

Last Christmas Kelly opened a present from his uncle, whose initials RAM appeared on the gift tag. "Do you know what that stands for?" Kelly's grandma asked.

"Of course!" he replied with confidence to spare. "Random access memory."

No longer satisfied with merely *running* programs, he's taken to *re*-programming them lately. Just for kicks, he changed the coding on a math game the other day. Now instead of the message box reading "Oops!" when an error is made, it says "You big dummy!"

And that aptly describes how I feel next to Bill—er—I mean, Kelly. I thought I had a fairly decent grasp of 'puter knowledge 'til he came along. As his homeschool teacher, I'm humbled on a daily basis.

His great ambition is to learn how to create programs. In the meantime, he's making plans to launch a computer tutoring business, having already starred in his own instructional video. But that won't happen 'til he's much older.

Like, say, ten.

NO PAIN, NO VAIN

SO I SHOW UP for class wearing the latest in fitness gear—spandex bodysuit, aerobically correct shoes and a sweatband thrown in for good measure. Thus adorned, I committed myself to a lesson in facersize.

Working out one's face is rather new to me, although a lady I saw on TV claims she's done it for years. "I started in my thirties and now I'm a hundred-something," she bragged, flaunting her youthful-looking mug before the camera.

"Oh, c'mon!" I hollered at the infomercial. "That babe ain't a day over twenty-one!" But a parade of before-and-after pictures convinced me otherwise.

So I looked into this newfangled concept and learned that for two hundred clams, I could attend a workshop that would teach me how to restore my youth. It demonstrates facial calisthenics for all sorts of trouble spots—gelatin jowls, a double chin, even a droopy eyelid that threatens to slam shut without warning. The workshop lasts about six hours or until someone dislocates her jaw, whichever comes first.

If anyone asked me, I'd have sworn facial building would be a piece of cake. I mean, how hard can it be to do a cheek press? Better than that, no one takes your measurements. No perky instructor carries on a conversation while sustaining an aerobic blur. And no one nags you about reaching that darn target heart rate.

Boy, was *I* wrong! Facial building tones all of the muscles in the face, and they get just as sore as their southern counterparts. Furthermore, it's messy. Many drills have you jamming your fingers in your mouth, which makes for a drooling workout.

In order to assess our facial needs, we're asked questions like, "Do you have thin skin?" I'm glad my husband wasn't there to answer that.

Facersize requires considerable coordination. For example, an exercise claiming to shorten your nose calls for pushing up on the tip of it with your index finger while simultaneously pulling your top lip down to your chin. We looked like a roomful of chimps.

So I may try a different approach. There's a facial building program that actually uses an electrical charge, but I've got a better idea. Next time I spot a thundercloud, maybe I'll jog outside and see what develops.

NO TIME FOR SHOWTIME

ARMED WITH A PILLOW and a wide assortment of snacks, I sat down to watch a show I taped the night before last. I indulge in this pastime, on average, every other leap year, so I strove for just the right atmosphere. And it *was*—right up 'til the tape went blank before the movie ended.

I hate it when I miss the big climax. If you ask me, the weekly TV listing should alert us less observant types when a show goes into extra innings. A neon box, maybe, with a listen-up type message like, Duh! This movie runs two-*and-a-half* hours. Then we'd know enough to record the whole flick and avoid viewus interruptus.

And another thing. If they'd cut out those hundred-and-one commercials, movies would finish on time. To combat this annoyance I fast forward through them but—oops!—go too far and miss the next scene. So I press the rewind button and—oops!—hurl it too far in the *other* direction. I'd save time and aggravation by simply watching the darn things, but can't bring myself to do that.

And why is it after making the effort to record a show, we rarely feel like watching it? We have a whole library full of videos we never want to see again.

"How 'bout *Gone With the Wind?*"

"Na."

"The *Blair Witch Project?*"

"Ho-hum."

"Jane Fonda's *High Impact Workout?*"

"Excuse me?"

Then on those rare occasions we get the urge to view one, we need a bloodhound to track it down. This makes a good argument for labeling tapes. I always *mean* to do that but, gee, who has the time?

To make matters worse, we often tape over prerecorded videos and fail to note the change. Later we plug in *You've Got Mail* only to see Martha Stewart baking her brains out.

Clearly, we've come a long way since the motion picture camera was invented, and this family has the disorganized tape library to prove it. I have to wonder what Thomas Edison would say. As our eight-year-old son pointed out, "If it wasn't for him, we'd see a blank screen when we turn on the TV."

On the other hand, maybe that wouldn't be so bad.

ON MY CHIT LIST

I'D BE PARALYZED if not for my daily To Do List. Not only does it remind me what needs to be done, but I derive great satisfaction from checking off each item. So much so that sometimes I cheat and write down things I've already completed.

This amuses my husband, Dan, who functions only in logical mode. He also razzes me about some of the items I include, like Take a shower.

"You could *forget* to do that?" he asked once.

"Of course not," I replied. "But I have 'to do' it, so it belongs on my To Do list. I also affectionately refer to it as a Chit List.

Grocery lists help me function, too. They itemize, in a cryptic sort of way, what's needed at the store—except for those products I'm too embarrassed to jot down. I mean, what if I run into people I know and they read over my shoulder? Or, worse yet, I could lose the list in some aisle and whoever found it would know instinctively that I'm the one buying Ex-Lax. No matter how well I hide the package.

Wish lists are far more fun to write than either of the above but they can result in severe writer's cramp. Hmmm...I want this...and that...and let's not forget *those*! Furthermore they're seldom taken seriously by our loved ones who think, *Oh, for heaven's sake, I can't buy* her that!

A friend relayed how she went to great lengths to describe the gift she wanted, how much it cost and where it could be purchased, but her husband bought her something else. This miffed her, but she refrained from violence, which brings to mind a less desirable type of roster.

Hit lists have grown in popularity, especially among the nation's school children. And while I find that situation appalling, it's heartening to know they practice their penmanship.

Less violent and far more entertaining are David Letterman's Top Ten Lists. He should make one itemizing the Top Ten Reasons we make lists.

One list I've never gotten around to making is a travel list. For ten-odd years I've packed blindly for trips to our summer shack, omitting this and forgetting that. Some day I'm gonna get my chit together and make a travel list to ease that problem.

Then maybe I can stay off my family's list.

ON THE Q-T (QUALITY TIME)

WE ALL KNOW the importance of quality time with our kids, and when we forget, the media is right there to remind us. This often results in turning an uneventful afternoon into a long-remembered fiasco.

The other day I read an article about Q-T and thought, We *should be having fun together*. "Let's bake cookies!" I announced, and my eight-year-old son agreed. He watched me cream butter, stir in eggs and add flour before speaking up.

"Don't I get to help?"

"Um...sure," I said, reluctantly handing him the spoon. "But try to keep everything in the bo—"

"Oops!"

"Kell, ya gotta be more careful!" I yelled, hauling out a stepladder. "Do you know how hard it is getting dough off a ten-foot ceiling?"

Despite my nagging, he stuck around 'til the first dozen came out of the oven. I tried everything short of a chisel, but they clung to the cookie sheet like leeches.

"Non-stick, my rump," I muttered.

"They taste good, though," Kelly said sampling a hacked-up specimen.

While I wrestled with the remainder, he snuck off to play on his computer.

Too often we parents concentrate more on the results than the occasion itself, and quality time gets lost in the shuffle. A friend told me about the year she helped her kids build a parade float. An impressive trophy was at stake, and what began as a fun project turned into fierce competition with her children's playmate.

"My Grandpa's making mine better than yours!" the little girl bragged.

"Oh yeah?" my pal said. "Well, ours is gonna win!"

Her daughters wisely stayed out of the debate, and in the end, someone *else's* float triumphed.

Complicating matters is the fact that quality time is so relative. Chances are, you and your kids have two entirely different ideas of how it should be spent.

"Why don't you watch me play pinball?" Kelly's suggested a time or two.

"No, no—the whole point is that we do something *together*."

"Okay," he counters. "Let's *both* watch me play pinball."

Furthermore, quality time can't be forced. I've tried that we're-gonna-play-this-game-and-have-*fun*-darn-it! method and it doesn't work. When my Number One Son is occupied, the best thing I can do is curl up on the couch with my well-meaning magazine.

And spend quality time with myself.

PICASSO WITHOUT A CANVAS?

A WHILE BACK I PAMPERED myself with one of those free makeovers you see advertised. The fake-up artist told me how to make my eyes look bigger and worked her magic on my malleable mug. When she finished, I hurried home to surprise my Better Half, who gazed at me and said, "What is this—Halloween? Go wash your face!"

This is not to say Dan likes his women plain. I still recall him splitting a gut the first time he saw me *au naturale*. Then he mumbled something about a rude awakening, but I couldn't hear with the bag on my head.

So to keep from amusing the general public, I put my face on before venturing outdoors. But there's a fine line between polishing our features and plastering the daylights out of them. And speaking of fine lines, I've noticed quite a few in the mirror lately. The dame has a few kilometers on the ol' kisser.

Luckily, she's wiser than the newlywed who, on a whim, bought some false eyelashes back in the mid-80s. I carefully applied adhesive and gently tapped them into place. As I went about my work, I practiced batting my eyes and failed to notice the lashes had loosened up. When my dear husband arrived home, he witnessed his first centipede duel.

Just for the record, neither survived and I buried their lifeless bodies in the trash. What I *really* need is false eyebrows anyway. Then I could dispense with painting the buggers on each day. I feel like Picasso without a canvas. The toughest part is drawing a mirror image. If they could curve in the same direction, no one would notice when I have two lefties.

Maybe it's operator error, but over the years I've acquired a makeup bag full of mistakes. Some of its contents include eye shadow that makes me look battered, and lipstick so bright it halts traffic. Then there's the foundation that, when applied as directed, alters my nationality.

You'd think I'd give up but, fact is, I *act* better if I look better, so I continue to cover the flaws as best I can. And oh by the way, I found out how to make my eyes look bigger *without* cosmetics.

It's called reading glasses.

RETURNING TO WOODSTOCK

I BOUGHT A HIGHLY SOPHISTICATED sound system in my twenties and soon amassed a sprawling collection of "reck-ords," as the Beatles would say. From hard rock to classical...from Abba to ZZ Top...whatever my mood, I had music to match. Then tragedy struck and my sound system died, as sound systems often do, leaving behind a hundred-and-fifty long-playing orphans.

After ten tuneless years, Dan and I had a meeting of the minds. Okay, okay—a hearing of the half-wits. At any rate, we decided the time was right for a musical investment. But why buy an ultra modern CD player when we're up to our eardrums in vinyl frisbees? So, with little fanfare, we bought some less popular components. (I could tell by the dusty boxes.) Then Dan masterfully hooked them up and soon we opened Carnegie Hall.

Our living room burst to life with voices we hadn't heard in ages. Bruce Springsteen...Huey Lewis... *Man, I'm hip!* I thought and cranked the volume, much to our eight-year-old's dismay.

"I'm just testing the acoustics," I said defensively.

My toe tapped wildly as the Monkees cried, "We're the young generation and we've got somethin' to say!" They certainly *looked* young on the album cover, but I suspect they're coping with hair loss by now. Not to mention middle-age spread.

I once knew every word of darn near every tune, but time has a way of deleting data like that. Luckily, many "reck-ord" companies included a sheet of lyrics so we rabid fans could sing along with our latest heartthrob. Anxious to harmonize, I scanned a few, only to find the type had shrunk considerably. So I swallowed my pride and chased down my bifocals.

Music magically transports us back in time. Each song stirs up images of people, places and events I hadn't thought of in years. Some melodies even bring a tear or two—like *Time in a Bottle* and *My Dingaling*. As a rule, though, I stick with upbeat tunes. Nothing against Barry McGuire but I've lost my ear for *Eve of Destruction*.

And if I'm in the mood for travel, I turn to Boston, Chicago or Little

Texas. But wherever the music takes me, you can bet I'm having fun and wish you were here.

SUPERSTITIOUS MINDS

I'M TAKING PRECAUTIONS to ward off bad luck this Friday the 13th. Nothing notably lousy ever happened in the past, but why tempt fate?

It's not that I'm overly superstitious. You won't see me toss a pinch of salt over my shoulder unless my order of fries is back there. However, I don't walk under ladders and feel likewise about scaffolding after bonking my head last summer.

There's a logical reason why I don't invite thirteen to dinner. We only own table service for eight and I'd hate to see a food fight break out.

Sure, I wince when a black cat crosses my path—especially if that path happens to be a highway. It won't improve my day and chances are it'll mess up her karma, too.

If I had a favorite number, it would be three. But most people I know prefer Lucky Number Seven and its fortuitous friend, Eleven. Following that mindset, a Port Huron couple married on the eleventh day of the seventh month. Their children from previous marriages participated, ranging in age from seven to eleven. And the nuptials took place at the local 7-Eleven. I guess that makes it a marriage of 'convenience.'

Still others think nine brings good fortune. On September 9, 1999, ninety-nine Malaysian couples took part in a mass wedding at 9:09 a.m. They were even *dressed* to the nines.

Personally, I'm more concerned with *bad* luck. After reading the *Dictionary of Superstitions* (author, David Pickering), I'm newly aware of situations to avoid. For instance, if I didn't realize it before, I officially now know it's bad luck to be hit by bird droppings. That explains why my car keeps breaking down.

For those who lean toward superstitious-ness, take these safeguards to avoid misfortune: Get out of bed on the same side you got *into* bed. Then dress starting with the right hand and right foot, but do *not* wear green.

Be sure to crack open the large end of your eggs. And don't, under any circumstances, let the chair fall when you sit down to breakfast. Head out the door with your right foot first. If your license plate numbers add up to thirteen, you might consider hoofing it to work—ever mindful of our feathered friends, of course.

Follow these precautions and you should emerge from Friday the

13th in pretty good shape.

As for me, I'm staying in bed.

TAKING A HIKE

I "RAN ACROSS" A book the other day called *How to Walk Your Way to Fitness* (D Lo Marketing). Not literally, of course. "Ran across" sounds like I exerted energy when, in fact, I parked my rump at the computer.

At any rate, the title struck me a bit odd. Let's be honest here. It's not a question of ignorance. ("Let's see...how do I walk my way to fitness? Should I start with the left foot or right?") But, hey, it offered a money back guarantee, so if some stooge reads it and *still* can't figure it out, he gets a refund.

Believe it or not, I used to log six miles a day. And, no, it wasn't uphill all the way, although it felt like it at first. I lost unsightly pounds—Are they ever "sightly"?—and soon wore sizes I hadn't spoken to since junior high. Too bad the pounds and I had a reunion after my stint ended.

No one called it "power walking" back then, but my activity may not have qualified anyway. Power walks involve flexed arm movements and hand-held weights. Although I never left home without my tunes, I would have felt downright silly taking my dumbbells for a hike.

Besides, I was stared at enough as it was. Drivers craned their necks as they rode by. You'd think they'd never seen a portable record player before. And every so often, some Good Samaritan stopped and asked if I wanted a lift.

"Sure!" I'd say, "Can you make me six inches taller?"

I get a kick out of watching others walk though. There's such a variety of techniques out there. Some people engage a practiced wiggle, while others have more of a strut. Some folks stride forward with great purpose, while others merely shuffle along. And though they each experience varying degrees of exercise, at least they're not rotting away at their PC.

Clearly, it's time to return to my long-abandoned walking program. So I'm hauling my trusty treadmill out of storage to prevent wiping out on the ice. I've never been in traction and don't plan to start now. To combat the boredom associated with indoor treks, I'm producing a video of things I typically encountered on outdoor walks: squirrels in the park...gawking drivers...dogs foaming at the mouth...

And I'll plunge right back into fitness—just as soon as I shut this thing off.

THE BIG HAIRY DEAL

WITHIN DAYS OF each other, two friends of mine suffered a similar trauma. At separate beauty shops, they received the 'Hairdo from H-E-Double-Bobby-Pins.' To make matters worse, they had to pay for the service when they felt more like suing someone's butt.

I can relate since I've been there and "do"-ed that. Fact is, we women are pretty particular about our hair. A crummy cut or a dire dye job, and we withdraw from society until it grows out.

By contrast, guys are pretty laid back about their "do." They go to the same shop, sit in the same chair, request the same cut and are indifferent to the whole process. Furthermore, they don't fight back tears when they get to the car or buy some goofy looking turban on the way home.

Another practice guys refrain from is primping before the appointment. How many women can make the same claim? What sense does it make to wash and style our bob as chicly as possible, only to be dunked in a sink moments later?

We should be far more concerned with having a bad hairdresser day. For starters, take a gander at your haircutter's head. Does it belong in *Hairdo* magazine or under a paper bag? If you're inclined to say, "Beautician, style thyself," it may be time to seek out a new one.

Some people spend their whole life in search of the perfect hairdresser, while others get snipped by the same scissors 'til they croak. Loyalty is a virtue, as long as it's for the right reason. No one should ditch the normally astute hairdresser for an occasional dud. But don't stay with someone "because I don't wanna hurt her feelings." What about your *hair*? It has feelings, too!

Like a visit to a fine restaurant, the service is as important as the end product, so consider the beautician's attitude. Is she congenial or does she act like she's doing you a whopping favor? Does she focus solely on your hair? Or does she flit from hither to yon while you imitate a drowned rat?

If so, you may want to shop around. Because when it comes to your mop, it *is* a big, hairy deal.

TO READ OR NOT TO READ

AS A COURTESY TO its customers, McDonald's provides a variety of newspapers. So I'm sitting there reading this compelling article, and what happens? The lady in the next booth turns the page. Of all the nerve! Now I get my *own* copy.

In fact, I get more than that. One of the perks of writing for newspapers is that most of them give me a free subscription. Determined to read them all before they hit the recycle bin, I've watched them multiply like mink.

For as long as I can remember, I've loved to read. I recall getting an eyeful at the grocery store as a wee lass. I dissolved into a fit of giggles after sounding out rump roast, much to my mother's embarrassment.

At age five, my first trip to the library filled me with awe. I checked out a stack of books that outweighed me and became a virtual expert on Dick and Jane. Though my reading material has changed over the years, the urge remains constant.

Trouble is, I have less time than ever to read. Consequently, I squeeze it in wherever possible—waiting in line...working out...in the Throne Room... One of my favorite reading nooks is the car. My husband, Dan, gets miffed if I have my nose in a book, though. Especially when I run off the road.

There's no lack of reading material, however, and swear I was a librarian in a previous life. A bulging bookcase graces every room of my home except the closets, though I've stuffed volumes in them as well. And I've vowed not to buy another magazine 'til I finish the tons I have.

My passion for pages finds me in good company. I read a biography claiming that Thomas Edison started at one end of his hometown library and read his way through every book. I'd like to see him try that on the Internet.

Elis Stenman was no slouch with reading material either. The Rockport, Massachusetts man made headlines in 1924 when he built a house out of newspapers. If that wasn't newsworthy enough, he made the furniture from paper logs. After all these years the house still stands, and visitors from all over the nation pay good money to read old news.

Inspired by this tourist attraction, I'm building a condo with *my* newspapers. And I'll let y'all know when it's ready.

UNFIT TO BE TIED

I RAN INTO A FORMER grade school chum who is considerably better preserved than I.

"Boy, have *you* changed!" she marveled.

I listened for an approving tone, but heard none. Then, as people do this time of year, I asked if she planned to attend her reunion.

"I doubt it," she replied. "All the jocks in my class are fat and balding now, but I can still fit into my majorette costume." Her body may be in shape, but her ego could stand to lose a few pounds.

Or maybe it's just sour grapes. For kicks, I hauled out last year's summer clothes and suffered grave disappointment. Somehow, in the last six months, every last one of them shrank. I needed two shoehorns just to squeeze into a pair of shorts. And after all that effort, the zipper held fast in a V-formation. Some cash lurked in one pocket, but even *that* didn't cheer me up.

After tugging them off, I repeated this sorry scene with the rest of my togs, mindful of the fact that, hey, they weren't just randomly plucked from a store rack. Once upon a time those babies fit! Even my faithful muumuu felt a little strained.

Feeling masochistic I took on the swimwear department. Besides, I was on a roll, if you'll pardon the pun. Out of a dozen stretchy Lycra suits, only the red and purple ones allowed entry (although most of me had to wait outside). So I faced the decision of whether to sunbathe as a stop sign or as Dino.

You'd think I'd learn by now. Each spring I vow to eat right and exercise so when summer comes along, I'll be a svelte, little number. But the only thing I end up losing is my resolve. More often than not, in fact, I *gain* weight. It's like somebody pulled my ripcord when I wasn't looking.

Meeting a slim but snooty former school chum only serves to remind me of my regression. But people who act superior like that should get a taste of their own medicine. Now that I've had a week to reflect, I've thought of a comeback to her boast about the majorette costume.

I should have said, "Oh, yeah? Well, I can still fit into my maternity clothes."

UNTIL THE NOVEL-TY WEARS OFF

"I HAVE THIS GREAT idea for a book," I told my friend, Kay, and briefly summarized the plot over the next two hours. "A best seller for sure," I concluded. "Oprah pick...movie rights...the whole nine yards..."

"So why haven't you written it yet?" she asked.

"Who has time?" I said, rattling off a list of personal commitments.

But our conversation echoed in my head until I vowed to draft the Great American Novel. Or a so-so book of dubious heritage.

The secret to accomplishing a major project like that is to break it down. To finish an eighty-thousand-word novel in a year, I'd have to write fifteen hundred words a week. Not counting weekends, that's three hundred words a day...divided by eight hours...that comes to one measly word every other minute! I'd only have to excuse myself five times while eating supper.

Having deciphered all that, I waited 'til the next morning to start the actual writing process. Dark and early I warmed up my computer as characters, setting and dialogue leaped and frolicked in my head. But when the blank screen appeared they ran for cover, scared off by that darn cursor.

I sat there for ten-odd minutes idly tapping my fingers on the keyboard. *Wait!* I thought, *a new writing project deserves a new diskette.* So I spent considerable time choosing a suitable color. After attaching a fancy label clearly titled "Novel," I thought, *Now I'm ready.*

But my stomach growled, reminding me of how starved I felt all of a sudden. After a quick bite to eat and a pit stop, I returned to my desk, determined to produce my quota.

'Once upon a time,' I typed furiously, before writer's block gripped me in its clutches again. I leafed through one of my writing guides and learned that stories can be written in any order desired. If a scene in the middle proves difficult, come back to it later. So I took that advice and typed the ending, '...and they lived happily ever after.'

I leaned back in the chair, satisfied with my efforts. Then I realized my novel contained only ten words. *Hmmm...maybe this would make a better short story,* I said to myself.

Many writers use a pen name, so I gave it some thought and came up with Bic. And that's what I'll be known as, until the novel-ty wears off.

WHAT'S MY (SON'S) LINE?

A SURVEY CONDUCTED by EPIC/MRA of Lansing revealed that parents have the greatest influence on their children's career selection. This comes as a big relief to me. I shuddered to think my son might really become a Tele-Tubby.

It may not be easy exerting my influence, however, and I base that theory on past experience. I intended, for instance, that Kelly would play for the Green Bay Packers. I briefed him on the finer points of football, dressed his room in green and gold, and bought him a pint-sized uniform. But he refuses to watch a game with me. He doesn't even qualify as a fair weather fan.

My second choice centers around the priesthood, which is experiencing a serious shortage these days. To solve that dilemma, some liberal groups pushed for married priests, but Pope John Paul put the kibosh to that idea. So along with offering spiritual fulfillment, this vocation would eliminate girl troubles, in-law conflicts and fights over the $%#!* thermostat. The only problems my son would assume would be those of a few thousand parishioners.

I could see a career in computer technology, too, since Kelly shows a smattering of knowledge in that area. I just wish he'd okayed it with me before reconfiguring my hard drive.

Naturally I'd encourage any profession that pays well and offers generous benefits. This includes acronym-type positions like a CPA, or a CEO of some high falutin' firm. But I'd discourage him from becoming a DPW (Disgruntled Postal Worker) because that field is already flooded.

These days, the career possibilities are endless. To help me decide what my son wants to be, I'm having him take a MAPP test. That stands for Motivational Appraisal of Personal Potential and it's a lengthy questionnaire designed to reveal one's occupational bent. I took it myself and got a D minus.

But it wasn't my fault! The quiz took forever and listed a zillion questions. For example, would you rather a) assemble a thousand-piece jigsaw puzzle, or b) work a crossword puzzle in the newspaper?

My choice would be: c) wait for the answers in the next day's edition, but that option wasn't listed.

I'm anxious for Kelly to finish the test so we can find out his life's work. If he's not retirement age by then.

YOU DON'T SAY

KIDS HAVE A UNIQUE way of describing things. I conjured up quite an image when I heard a little girl say, "The grossest thing I ever throwed up was pizza."

Although my eight-year-old hasn't expanded on that particular subject, he renders an opinion on other important topics. Always open about his feelings, I remember the time he gushed, "I love you more than magnets or electricity or *anything*. And for *sure* I love you more than taking a bath."

Never too fond of that activity, he routinely spews out reasons for not needing one. "But I just had a bath last week!" he said once.

One day, I introduced him to a new toothpaste I hoped would tempt him to brush longer. When I asked how he liked it he shook his head in disgust. "*Chocolate* mint is the kinda mint I'm into."

One time, my pint-sized son told me he had a big butt. "I wish *I* had a big butt like that," I said.

"You *do* have a big butt, Mom," he replied.

I chuckled at his reaction to a holiday newsletter we got with a typo that read, *Merry Christmars!* "I guess the second 'R' is silent," he mused.

Normally a good speller, he wrote a note fraught with errors. When I asked why, he said, "I'm spelling words wrong on purpose so my friend can read it."

He likes inventing things and once built a 'Love Giver.' "It's small enough to fit in your pocket, so when I'm not around, I can still give you my love."

When I served his favorite meal a while back, he told me, "I'm sure glad I picked you for a mom. I didn't know how it was gonna work out at first."

But now I've passed inspection, he's the last word in loyal. One evening, I griped when he snuck off after I announced bedtime.

"Nag, nag, nag," my husband, Dan, said.

"Mom is *not* a nag!" Kelly replied. "For the thousandth time!"

I'm glad he's still young enough to share his fantasies with me. An avid pinball player, he breathlessly told me about a dream he had. "I dreamt I took the glass off Twilight Zone and could do anything I wanted to the playfield!"

But he's growing too quickly and some day I'll have to be satisfied with my cardboard 'Love Giver.' And my ever-growing book of quotes.

CHAPTER TWO - CAN THIS MARRIAGE BEHAVE?

ALL PUCKERED OUT

I ENJOYED THE INNOCENT kiss my husband and I shared. But as he walked away, he wiped his mouth with the back of his hand. Where exactly is the romance in that? Back when we courted, a kiss was a cherished commodity. Now it's just one more thing to clean up after.

I'll never forget my first kiss—and neither will the suave nine-year-old whose glasses I knocked off. Hey, it wasn't intentional! I just panicked when I saw his face move in on me. A second attempt convinced him to find someone more experienced. So there I sat all brokenhearted.

Things could have gone much smoother if the Internet had been around then. I stumbled over a web site the other day that sets forth basic kissing tips. These include such pointers as brushing your teeth (so your partner doesn't pass out). And closing your eyes. (Wait 'til just before your lips meet to avoid injury.) Furthermore, people who use that French method, take heed…you don't earn extra credit for probing your partner's esophagus.

My favorite author, Gregory J.P. Godek, offers some creative suggestions on the subject in his book, *1001 Ways to be Romantic*. But for the full poop, one should read *The Art of Kissing* by William Cane. This is an all-encompassing guide that expands on such little-known techniques as the Vacuum Kiss. I'd draw the line on that one. No matter how much I relish my Hoover, I feel a handshake is sufficient.

How long should a kiss last? That depends on the parties' desire. Last year, an Israeli couple desired to win a marathon kissing contest so they puckered up for an incredible thirty hours and forty-five minutes. Although they had to be treated for fatigue, they won $2,500 cash and a trip around the world. All things considered, I'd say they 'made out' pretty well.

So what happens if you lack a significant other? Call Rover over! Loads of people smooch their pooch on a regular basis. James B. Miller, D.V.M., says, "Obviously, it's not really a sanitary thing to do...but you probably won't get anything from (it)." True, dogs can transmit strep throat, but so can humans. And canines are way more loyal.

If Woody the Beagle were still around, I'd give it a try. But with my luck, he'd wipe his mouth with the back of his paw.

BROODING OVER BATHROOM BEEFS

SO I STEP OUT of the shower to find the bathroom door agape and an arctic blast pouring in. Shivering, I dry myself off in haste before stomping out to confront my groom of eighteen years.

"Why must you leave that door open?" I shriek for the dozenth time.

"Because you're wrecking the plaster," Dan replies for the dozenth time. He escorts me back to the steam room, and calls attention to the telltale cracks overhead.

"I don't care if the ceiling caves in!" I yell. "I wanna be warm!" At this point, I threaten to flush the commode when he's in the shower, and thus goes another round in an all-too-familiar feud.

Our bathroom hosts the battleground for other squabbles, too. Sometimes I fail to push down the shower release knob after my daily sprinkle. The water left in the pipes turns decidedly chilly, thus surprising the next human to take a shower. That, of course, would be Dan, whose rugged dialogue invariably clues me in.

I haven't personally experienced this bathroom beef of his and he can't relate to mine. But we *both* grind our teeth over another situation: finding two squares of bath tissue on the roll for a twenty-square job.

But even a full dispenser can cause personal anguish. We use one of those spring-loaded types that nestles in its cradle just so. All heck breaks loose if it's even a dab off kilter. The slightest touch sends it clanging to the floor and bun wad romping around the room. When this annoying spectacle occurred more often than not, I consulted my eight-year-old son, who'd thought it made a great practical joke. I beg to differ.

Kelly's latrine habits reversed themselves over the last year. Prior to that, he avoided it so much I thought he had a porcelain allergy. Now he's resident Bathroom Hog even while away from home. My friend, Connie, felt the need to investigate when her daughter and my son spent a suspicious chunk of time in her powder room. But she relaxed when she found them making faces in the mirror.

Things could get worse. According to a survey conducted by American Standard, by the time Kelly turns eighteen, he may spend an hour or more a day in the bathroom. And those making faces will be his disgruntled parents.

CAN THIS MARRIAGE BEHAVE?

SHORTLY AFTER GUTENBERG invented the printing press, *Ladies Home Journal* began publishing a regular article called "Can This Marriage be Saved?" According to *LHJ*, it's "the most popular, most enduring woman's magazine feature in the world." Why? Because there's nothing dysfunctional couples like better than reading about *other* dysfunctional couples.

These stories of warring wedlock are quite a contrast to the *Little House on the Prairie* rerun I saw the other day. The episode depicted the Ingalls family pulling up stakes and enduring all manner of unpleasantries in its move to Kansas. No matter what hare-brained idea Charles came up with, his dutiful wife Caroline went along with it.

Charles: "Let's cross this swollen, raging river in a wobbly covered wagon even though we could all drown."

Caroline: "Whatever you think, Charles."

I wanted to yell, "Gosh, have some backbone, lady!"

Or maybe she had the right idea. As I recall, they didn't bicker much in that series. When conflicts arose, Caroline busied herself by churning butter or washing clothes without benefit of a Maytag. Later, Charles would apologize, blink back a few of those manly tears of his and all was forgiven.

Not so in this house. I hate like heck to suffer in silence. In fact, things reached a fevered pitch a while ago and I knew something had to change. So I read this helpful guide called *Lasting Promise* (Scott Stanley, author)—sort of a marriage-counselor-in-a-book type of thing.

The first section dealt with handling conflicts, something we enjoy on a regular basis around here. It showed examples of imaginary discussions that can occur when disputes arise. I got the distinct feeling they'd eavesdropped on us. It also gave examples of positive dialogue that could be substituted. Somehow I can't picture myself in the heat of battle saying, "Okay, honey, now it's *your* turn to have the floor."

The book also offers exercises to do. Not aerobic ones, thank heaven, but practical steps to take in order to resolve future conflicts— things like establishing ground rules and analyzing each other's answers to the nosey questions in the book.

I finished *my* exercises weeks ago. Now if I could just get *Dan* to do his part, we'd know if this marriage can behave.

DIETARY DEMENTIA

"YOU'RE COUNTING THE calories in my sandwich, aren't you?" Dan asked as he bit off a chunk.

"What makes you think that?" I answered, the picture of innocence.

"I can tell by the look on your face," he replied between chews.

He was right, of course. One can't diet without becoming a little obsessed. And tallying other people's food is more fun than counting my own. Let's see, I pondered as he munched away...two slices of bread, cheese, lunchmeat, a dollop of mayo...

"Holy cow!" I yelled. "You just blew six hundred calories!"

I could tell he cared by the blank stare that greeted me.

Calorie counting causes conundrums, too. Not all foods list nutritional information. When I try to estimate, I'm way off base like some loser on *The Price is Right*. I've been known to go to great lengths to get an accurate figure. The other day I was "thisfar" from calling the Pope about communion hosts.

(Drum roll, please.) Enter Calorie Control Council at www.caloriecontrol.org. (End with cymbal crash.) This web site features a list of calorie counts for everything on the planet and other assorted data. That's all well and good, but do we *really* want to boot up our computers each time we eat a morsel? Furthermore, we still have to weigh and measure food to know how much an ounce is. And how accurate is a kitchen scale that states, Not Legal for Trade?

What exactly *is* a calorie anyway? Let's get technical for a minute. Calorie is short for kilocalorie, one of which will raise the temperature of one kilogram of water by one degree Centigrade. So if calories are units of heat, how come I pull on a sweater after every meal?

And how many kilocalories should we kill? That depends on how much we want to weigh. Your average, moderately active adult needs fifteen calories to maintain a pound. So, theoretically, those who yearn to be a hundred-pound weakling could eat as much as fifteen hundred calories daily—preferably not in one sitting. Granted, the weight would come off slowly, but Pompeii wasn't lost in a day. Or was it? I forget.

Another thing you should 'lose' is your scale. To keep it from discouraging you, store it somewhere out of reach. Like the roof.

After following this eating plan for a month, my ring twirls more loosely than before. Now if I can just get my belt to do that...

EAT, DRINK AND BE WARY

THE ROOM MOST likely to host an argument in our house has to be the kitchen. We eat our meals at a rustic little booth, and the close quarters bring each other's dining habits clearly into focus.

My Better Half prefers his food at room temperature, although he *has* devoured entire meals right from the fridge. But cook him a nice hot dinner and he bristles. Then he blows on it for ten-odd minutes while I, sitting across from my beloved, am blasted by hurricane winds.

"Would you mind?" I said the other day.

"Mind what?" Dan asked, concentrating on the matter at hand.

"Blowing in another direction!"

"Well, at least I don't scrape the fork across my teeth like you do," he replied.

"The heck I do," I said, scraping the fork across my teeth.

You don't wanna eat at our house. We tend to be uncouth at times. Good manners would have us munch the recommended thirty-six bites, swallow and then speak a few polite words. But, more often than not, we chat while we chew, gulp and stuff more in. So much for diction. Furthermore, our elbows rest firmly on the table unless we're picking our teeth. We should invite Miss Manners over just for yuks.

I found no mention of these habits in my tasteful copy of *Emily Post on Entertaining*. However, it does describe the proper way to set a table as well as the function of each utensil. Apparently, I've been remiss all these years. Up 'til now, I ate every course with a shrimp fork. Oh, the shame of it.

Still, I strive to prepare nutritious foods that are pleasing to the eye. But then Dan downs something bizarre like stew with ketchup and the rest of us lose our appetites. "Don't insult my food," Dan says defensively between bites as we struggle with waves of nausea.

Refrigerator meals trigger another bone of contention. I have this aversion to family members drinking straight from the milk carton. Good thing we don't own a cow.

It's the same with leftovers. Dan wonders how I always know he ate from the bowl, but those little fork tracks are a dead giveaway.

Perhaps it's just as well. Vittles not smidgeoned away often get forgotten 'til well past their prime. Thus, our snacking motto has become eat, drink and be wary.

GO, GO, GO-CART!

I SMILED LAST spring when my husband, Dan, announced his next project: a go-cart for our son, Kelly. Ever since Grog invented the wheel, countless little boys—and full-grown ones—have dreamed of building the primitive vehicles. But in the end, they all look pretty much alike with their wooden chassis, four shaky tires and a piece of twine for wishful steering.

Dan spent the next month or so in his garage, emerging now and then to replenish his supply of brew. Meanwhile, Kelly eagerly awaited his toy.

"What's taking so long?" I asked in early June.

"I still have to rig up an ignition switch," Dan replied.

"Ignition switch?" said I. "What kinda go-cart *is* this anyway?"

I found out soon enough. Days later, he unveiled a mini dragster with a shiny, blue, welded frame, flotation tires, and a gleaming three-and-a-half horsepower engine. It featured forward, neutral and reverse gears, a padded seat and independent front suspension.

What? No radio?

I re-attached my eyeballs and expressed a few concerns.

"*This* is for an eight-year-old?" I shrieked.

"Yeah, but it's adjustable," Dan said proudly. "See? We can pull the seat back when he gets older."

"You mean *if* he gets older," I replied. "That sucker looks downright deadly."

"Wrong," he said defensively, as he tinkered with the brake pedal. "This thing is perfectly safe."

"Is that so? Well, then, why does it have a roll bar?"

Dan let out a deep, I'm-dealing-with-a-moron sigh. "That's just for effect, okay?"

"Fine," I said. "But what speed will Kelly be cruising in this thing?"

"Just fast enough to outrun his mother," Dan muttered.

All told, it took six weeks to build The Monster and, in keeping with my hubby's rather frugal nature, it cost just shy of a hundred bucks. But the labor of love wasn't without its problems, and Dan admits the air in his workshop turned royal blue at times.

"Because of the spray paint," Kelly explained.

"Indubitably," I agreed.

Frustration faded from memory when Test Drive Day arrived. Kelly drove his go-cart down the sidewalk with his trusty pit crew on either side. The noise attracted a parade of kids and I have to admit I enjoyed the spectacle.

Next stop: Daytona.

LIFE IN THE TRASH LANE

WE HAVE A CHRONIC argument in this house. Each week, we go head to head over something my Better Half throws away. Nothing is sacred. Acting as judge and jury, he decides the fate of whatever he encounters, regardless of ownership, and exiles it to the trash. If I'm lucky, I find it dripping with raw egg guts in the garbage can. More likely, it's hanging out at the city dump.

Okay—maybe I deserve it at times. I confess I don't always put things in their proper place, but neither does Dan. More than once I've plucked his dirty socks off the floor. If he's nearby I hear, "Don't take those. I wanna wear 'em again."

Furthermore, many items he's deported weren't just lying around. He tosses stuff from inside cupboards, too, which explains my topless Tupperware. And once he threw away some cookies I baked, "because no one was eating them."

"How do you know?" I asked, "Did you have twenty-four-hour surveillance on the jar?"

"No."

"Then ya shoulda left 'em alone!" I hollered.

It's gotten to the point that, when something disappears, I immediately suspect Dan of foul play. "Did you throw out my recipe for meatloaf?" I ask in an accusing tone of voice.

And he replies, "Of course not!" while trying to recall if he did.

I know the mental reasoning behind this annoying habit of his. *She'll never miss it,* he thinks to himself, and it *does* take awhile before I realize something's vanished. When reality hits, I pop a gasket. "I oughta throw *you* away!" I've squawked a number of times.

But that would be hard for a confirmed packrat like me. I have a devil of a time parting with *anything. Okay,* I think to myself. *maybe I haven't used this in over a decade, but who's to say I won't need it next week?*

To make matters worse, I tend to acquire more than one of things I greatly value. Take, for example, the new encyclopedia I just bought for a song. My fifth set. Because you can never have too many.

Chances are, Dan's hatching a plan to dump the other four, despite my recently imposed law of "Before you toss, ask The Boss." And then we'll find ourselves back in the ring.

MIDDLE AGE MUSING

HAVE YOU NOTICED that young people and those over eighty have something in common? They both like birthdays. As a rule, the younger the child, the prouder he is of his age, and ditto with older folks. Unlike the rest of us who skirt the issue, the aforementioned parties even toss the number into casual conversation. "I can ride a bike and I'm only five years old!" or "I can *still* ride a bike and I'm eighty-five!"

What a healthy outlook! Too bad most of us between forty and eighty don't possess the same mindset. Creeping up on middle age, I find my approaching birthday as welcome as razor burn. Somehow I can't picture myself gushing, "And I'm only forty-four!"

One of my best friends turned ninety this year. It didn't faze her a bit—and well it shouldn't. Many of the dozens of pals she acquired in nearly a century showed up to help her celebrate, and she charmed them all with her wit and grace.

I can imagine myself in that position. There I'd sit with shoulders slumped as revelers showed up bearing gifts. Like Lurch, the mirthless butler from the *Addams Family*, I'd groan and shake my head slowly from side to side.

Maybe those perched on the edges of age are content because we view them differently than ourselves. We tend to marvel at people like Grammy-winning country singer LeAnn Rimes, who heightened her fame by publishing a novel at age fifteen. Then that sorry underachiever went on to star in the subsequent movie. And who isn't equally impressed by the eighty-some-year-old woman who hobbles up to receive her diploma?

But more likely, it's because *they* see things differently. To children, life is a blank book waiting to be written in, and many folks past their prime vow to make the very most of that last chapter. Meanwhile, the rest of us wade through life as though it was a drawn-out Michener novel.

What we middle-aged masses need to do is change our way of thinking. The glass is half full and all that rot. The obits teem with people our age, so why not celebrate the fact we're not listed?

When the next birthday arrives, we should cherish it like children and savor it like seniors. And maybe even go for a bike ride.

MONEY FOR NOTHIN' AND YOUR CHECKS FOR FREE

I COULD RELATE TO the presidential election ordeal—the headache and heartache of checking and rechecking figures. I go through the same thing with my bank statement each month.

On one fickle finger I can count the number of times I balanced on the first try. Usually I cipher and re-cipher every transaction on a calculator the size of Tom Thumb. Sure, I have a standard desk model, but why haul it out for a quick job like that?

Ideally, check registers contain the date, payee, amount and number of each transaction, but I don't always take time to enter the vitals. More likely I'm swayed by that mile-long line of homicidal people behind me. *I'll record this check later*, I think, that being the last thought I have on the subject.

Sometimes I leave the payee blank to avoid getting the third degree from my Better Half. This gives the impression I was pressed for time instead of watching The Shopping Channel again.

But all heck breaks loose when one of us forgets to record a transaction entirely, especially since our balance routinely flirts with zero. Flipping through the register, I see a telltale gap in the numbering sequence. "Hey!" I holler at Dan. "What did you write number nine-forty-six out for?" As if he could remember. For surely it couldn't have been *me*.

Buying designer checks allows us consumers to make a personal statement. Unfortunately, they cause their share of trouble in this house. I don't care to have fish swimming on them, and Dan feels the same about cutesy kittens. If safety paper were our only option, we'd duke it out over the color.

What I don't understand is how a few hundred pieces of paper can cost so much. I like those introductory offers from check-printing companies vying for our business. They promise money for nothin' and your checks for free (or close to it). But after the initial order, you pay through the nose. Consequently, we play Musical Check Printing Companies on a regular basis.

Too regular. As one of those annoying shoppers who never carries cash, I write *lots* of checks. The canceled ones used to be returned by bulk mail. But we changed checking account services to avoid fees and earn microscopic interest. Now our canceled checks are shredded and recycled into something more useful.

Like bath tissue.

NO CANNING DO

MY BETTER HALF and I debated whether to plant a garden this spring.

The plot we forged a few years back is roughly the size of a grave and has seen about as much life. It did, however, provide for a Three "Beans" Salad one season—that being the sum total of its harvest.

I was so sure last year would be different. A seed we sowed grew into a snake-like vine, and after weeks of suspense, an itty bitty pumpkin began to grow. I planned to tell relatives after the first trimester, but by then it showed signs of decay.

This, despite hordes of attention lavished upon it. Not only did I spray it faithfully with the hose, but I talked to it as well. "Aw, wook at da witto pumpkin!" I gushed, offering it daily encouragement. But the pep talks turned to chiding and, eventually, I resorted to the silent treatment.

We tossed out the melon-sized ball of rot with more questions than answers. Did it have too much water? Sun? Air? Or maybe it would have thrived in a better location. Like Martha Stewart's garden.

Dan, our resident auto parts guy, suggested we abandon the grave-garden and sink a tire into the ground instead. "Whitewall side down, of course."

"Why would I want to plant veggies in a tire?" I asked.

"To keep the moisture in."

"Correct me if I'm wrong," I said, "but didn't moisture cause our pumpkin's demise?"

I found the answer in an article by Peter Bowden, a New York gardener with twenty years' experience playing in dirt. He says that spray watering is the "worst possible thing you can do to your plants." TV ads that show people out misting their gardens are a bunch of cow manure. (The ads, not the people.)

In truth, wetting leaves creates an ideal setting for fungus to grow among us. If you don't believe me, check my crisper. Not only that, cold water can shock plants. (When's the last time you showered with the hose?) Furthermore, spray watering washes the pollen off flowers, which means no visits from amorous bees and, ultimately, no harvest. And without produce to preserve, no canning do.

The solution, says Mr. Bowden, is to direct water into the soil, not over the plants. Based on his advice, we're taking one last stab at gardening.

I just hope he's not all wet.

A REMOTE CHANCE

IF MY MARRIAGE ever broke up, the custody battle would rage on for years. In the end, we'd be ordered to share all decisions affecting it. Hmmm...on second thought, I currently have darn little say over the TV remote.

I'm not sure when the conflict started, but gone are the days my husband, Dan and I snuggled on the couch watching some mutually agreeable program. Now he reigns on his rocking-chair throne with a death grip on the remote. And my viewing pleasure lies at the mercy of his trigger thumb.

Click

"What'd ya do that for?" I squawk. "I *liked* that other show!"

"Nag, nag, nag."

Click "White House aides have announced that President Bush will...*click*...suffer from painful, itching hemorrhoids...*click*...with a slight chance of...*click*...ring around the collar."

"Will you kindly knock it off?" I say. "My brain can't focus that fast."

It wouldn't be so bad if Dan would light on a channel for more than two seconds. But who knows if these programs might somehow transform our lives when he races past them in a blind fury?

"Those are just commercials," Dan says, dismissing my shrieks.

"Well, maybe I *like* commercials. Did you ever stop to think about *that*?"

"It's a guy thing," Dan explained one time. "We know exactly what we're looking for and aren't distracted by all that other garbage."

"Well, it distracts *me*," I grumbled.

He has a point though. Over the last year, I've noticed our Number One Son exhibiting the same trait—as if one power-hungry remote-controller in the family wasn't bad enough. Kelly skillfully maneuvers his way past shows like *Oprah* in search of the computer channel, slamming on his brakes for car-related ads.

Besides causing family conflicts, remotes shoulder the blame for viewers being flabby. Imagine how fit we'd all be if we stood up to change channels. But wait! Come to think of it, before remotes existed, I watched whatever mindless show came on after my favorite mindless show if I was too lazy to shut off the set.

That aside, on those rare occasions I clutch the remote in my hot, little hand, I savor the feeling of control that little device brings. My biggest kick comes from studying each channel at my leisure without hearing a chorus of groans.

Will I ever watch a whole program? Chances are pretty remote.

A ROYAL PAIN

MY GROOM AND I tumbled into one of those men-versus-women debates the other day. It all started when I told him about a crick in my neck.

"Women always complain about their health," Dan griped. "If it's not one thing, it's something else. And they *still* outlive their husbands."

"Hey, now!" I said, getting my dander up. "Guys are every bit as verbal about their aches and pains. Why, just this morning you grumbled about...er...what was that again?"

Hard as I tried, I couldn't recall the particulars, so I came up with a plan. Each time one of us voiced a medical complaint we'd mark it on the calendar. Then whoever had the highest score at the end of the week would be dubbed Head Hypochondriac. And said Royal Pain would receive a crown trimmed with Band-Aids.

"What colors should we use to keep track?" Dan asked.

"How 'bout black and blue?" I joked.

Now when one of us said, "It hurts when I do this," the other skipped the punch line and made a beeline for the calendar. It took a focused effort not to voice our ailments and we'd often catch ourselves in the middle of a gripe. ("Not tonight, dear. I have a huh—hotdog.")

Still we were pretty diligent that first day. I suffered in silence from a wrenching charley horse and Dan kept his blazing heartburn to himself. But he earned a point the next morning when he cussed out his sinuses for causing a sneezing fit. And I won a tally mark for whining over a paper cut.

It would be different if we had some life threatening illness—something for which symptoms should be noted and acted upon. But our petty complaints serve no real purpose. And if they continued unchecked, we'd age into those crotchety geezers people go to great lengths to avoid.

So who won the Royal Pain contest? Alas, it was a draw. But we racked up far more points than expected and our little experiment drove home the fact that we *both* bellyache too much.

I noticed, too, that when we can't gripe about our health, it's hard to think of something else to say. Then again, maybe that's good.

At any rate, I'm glad the week is over. All that effort gave me a serious headache.

SURFING THROUGH CB-SPACE

FOR A WHILE WE enjoyed communication between home and Camp Corky, but then the string snapped out of our paper cups. Someone suggested citizens band radios, the Internet of the Seventies. So, while the rest of the world surfed through cyberspace, we took a giant step backward.

"Breaker one-nine!" I said, brushing up on my long-abandoned CB slang.

A full quarter century ago, I rode the airwaves for fun and excitement. I met an interesting blend of people, but all of us had one thing in common: we talked funny.

CBers have their own distinct vocabulary. Nearly everyone knows "bears" refer to cops, thanks to the movie, *Smokey and the Bandit*. And the song *Convoy* made even city slickers feel like a Big Rigger. But only hundred-percent, dyed-in-the-wool CBers know that "breaking wind" does *not* mean you-know-what (although one needs gas to do it).

In addition, the Ten Code sets forth a verbal shorthand for all types of common phrases. For instance, "That's a big ten-four," is much quicker to say than "yes."

Anxious to become Good Buddies, we found a couple of old base units and ordered some far-reaching "fishing poles." You'd think antennas would come with the necessary hardware to install them, but no. After umpteen trips to the store, "we" (as in my husband) went to work. He scaled great heights to set up a base at home and the shack. As is customary, the two-hour project lasted most of a weekend.

Finally came the moment of truth. For nearly an hour we hollered to each other without success. I heard two Spanish-speaking dudes from heaven-knows-where, but not a sound from my spouse twelve scant miles away. Undaunted, he dismantled his station, putzed with it a while and, before long, we gave it another shot. It sounded rather faint, but this time I heard his voice. "Watson, come here! I need you!" (or something to that effect).

That first communication had the acoustic quality of a fast food speaker, which explained my craving for fries. Nevertheless, we chatted a spell amid raucous interference.

Now that we officially have our ears on, we Corcorans need to come up with names for ourselves. "Handles," as they're called, should reflect the personality of the CB users.

Thus we're leaning heavily toward Larry, Moe and Curly.

TOO MANY COOKS SPAR IN A BRAWL

LIKE MOST MARRIEDS, my husband and I perform selected tasks to keep our household running smoothly. Over the years, however, we've learned not to trespass on the other's chore list or suffer dire consequences.

I've made it my job, for instance, to push the vacuum around when carpet crud reaches a climax. And when Dan tiptoes into my territory, I threaten to siphon him with the Hoover. *His* job, as head of the maintenance department, is to keep the machine humming, despite the tangle of hairballs it ingests.

Dan also takes out the garbage and, in fact, forbids me to do it. He claims it's an exact science for which I have little aptitude. I'd disagree, but I don't much care for the task anyway.

Frankly, I'd rather handle the laundry that spawns in our bottomless hamper. When Dan 'helps out' by throwing in a load, I find it two days later clinging to the washer and sporting fungus.

Furthermore, I wash the dishes myself since I'm less likely to shatter them into sharp, little pieces. Dan has this habit of shaking them in the sink to dispel excess water and—*smash!*—they're history. "Hey, it's not *my* fault," he says in answer to my glare.

"Of course not," I reply. "The sink is a cereal-bowl killer."

For the most part I make like Julia Child when we're home on the range, but Dan vehemently insists on fixing meals at our getaway shack. One fracas in particular taught me that too many cooks spar in a brawl.

Dan also reigns over the indoor foliage department due to my gross incompetence in that area. He nurses our one and only plant, whose species is anyone's guess. Meanwhile, I water our sorry excuse for a garden each summer (or at least until the thrill of the first planting wears off).

And though I program the VCR, I know not how to reset its clock, so Dan rules when one of us blows a fuse. And trust me—it happens often in this house.

TOTALLY UNRECALLED

WHEN MY BETTER HALF quizzed me as to his social security number, I casually rattled it off.

"That's not *mine*," Dan said, a bit miffed. "It's your ex-husband's!"

Oops! I thought. Never a strong suit, my memory messes up more than ever lately. I've even forgotten what the show *Total Recall* was about.

This affliction runs in the family, as demonstrated by a distant relative of mine—okay, okay, she just *wishes* she was distant. Anyhow, she drove to her sister's house to visit and forgot to shut off her car. Luckily no one hijacked it, but the gas gauge took a serious nosedive.

Judging from all the memory-enhancing products on the market, most people draw a blank more than they care to admit. It's tempting to try solving the problem with, say, a regular dose of ginkgo. But a number of techniques can help us name that tune without forking out a cent. To improve that rarely accessed memory, give these proven methods a try:

1. Rote memorization—By saying or writing something over and over, you have a better chance of remembering it. That explains why I can still recite, "In the future I shall endeavor to create an atmosphere conducive to the learning process in Mr. Danforth's eighth grade history class."

2. Mnemonic Devices—These are mental images you conjure up to help remember words or phrases. The more bizarre the visual, the better. For example, to remind yourself what to buy at the grocery store, you might picture a chicken smoking a pickle.

3. Expanding Acronyms—Invent a silly phrase using the initials of words you need to remember. My eight-year-old guffaws at the term I came up with to recall tooth names. Incisors, canines, bicuspids and molars became 'I Can Bite Me.'

4. Song Sung New—Change the lyrics to a simple tune to reflect the desired knowledge. You may grow to hate the song, but the message will live eternally.

5. Note taking—Write in blood, if need be. Any surface will do. If no paper is available, jot down crucial info on your hands. My husband, Dan, often does this when he's on the road. I grew suspicious the day I found a finger with someone's phone number on it.

By practicing these techniques, I'll be ready next time Dan asks me his social security number.The answer is 9-1-1! Er—I mean, pi equals 3.14! No, wait! Thirty days hath September...

TWENTY-YEAR-OLD HOME WRECKER

IF YOU'VE FOLLOWED this column for the past eight years, you know about Lurch. My husband Dan's former fetish, Lurch, was a homely, clamorous rust-bucket that passed for a '68 Chevy van. For fourteen years,

I watched in disbelief as he pampered that eyesore and wrung out mile after mile. As faithful as he is to vehicles, I thought Lurch would be with us forever.

Then along came Big Red. One look at the '83 Dodge Ram and my fickle mate was smitten. He stood back to admire her nineteen-year-old body and eyed up her rear end. Then he forked out a hundred bucks and mounted her for the ride home. From then on, he casually discarded Lurch and me.

Big Red instantly became his obsession. "Let's go for a walk," I'd suggest, to get his mind off her.

But he'd mutter something about modifying her engine and that's the last I'd see of him. Another time he used the old I've-gotta-fix-her-transmission-selector-indicator line. Any excuse to be with her. He's spent countless dollars on this younger model, too, bringing her nice things to wear like mud flaps and a seat cover.

And you'd better believe she enjoys the attention. More than once I've caught her admiring herself in her new side mirrors. She knew darn well he installed the speakers to set the mood when they're together. I'm sure she'd blow her own horn if she could.

Then again, there's no need. Her suitor constantly brags to friends about how well she 'performs.' Thanks to more groping under her hood, he upped her mileage thirty percent. Big deal. So what if she gets twenty-three miles to the gallon on the highway? She belongs on a street corner if you catch my drift.

Always a stickler for regular maintenance, Dan's raised his standards considerably. He changes her oil every five miles or five minutes, whichever comes first. And each week, he's out there with the hose washing her all over—*even underneath.* I can just imagine what the neighbors think.

My estranged husband used to avoid cameras. So I knew things were serious when he asked me to take a picture of them together. I guess he keeps it in his wallet.

As for Lurch, he was forced to pack his bags and move out.

I can only hope I'm not next.

AN UNHAPPY MEDIUM

MY BUDDY, KAY, tapes a show for me on the Sci-Fi Channel called *Crossing Over.* It features John Edward, who is a medium, although I rate him higher than that. According to the promotional ad, when the dead talk, they talk to him. Consequently, those with vital signs pay big bucks to listen.

An audience of people packs into the gallery for each episode. During a typical show, John delivers personal messages to a few lucky spectators and plays back tapes of private readings. He tells those involved not to anticipate who might come through, but they always do. Many hope to reunite with a departed mother or child, but it's just as likely a dead but still obnoxious acquaintance will crash the party.

Private readings often involve celebrities. These lend credence to John's ability because, hey, if a famous actress (who makes her living pretending) says it happened, it must be true.

Regardless of who receives the message, I find myself completely wrapped up in it. I cry right along with them and honk my nose loudly. And I gasp when they gasp over details only a loved one could know. But the eerie coincidences and Twilight-Zone-ish music have no effect at all on my husband, Dan, the resident skeptic.

I convinced him to watch a show with me once. He sat there reluctantly as a notice flashed on the screen and a highly credible voice said, "What you are about to see is real. No information is given to John Edward about those he reads."

"Yeah, right," Dan muttered under his breath.

Nevertheless he listened to the first segment without comment. That is, until John assured the woman, "Just know that your deceased sister is okay."

"What does *that* mean—she's okay?" Dan asked. "She's dead, for Pete's sake!"

Nevertheless, he stuck around for another reading. Again, John Edward relayed highly detailed information about the souls who made contact. Names...dates...causes of death... possessions they left behind.... Everything but a social security number. Then he ended with, "They're pulling their energy back."

"Just in time for a commercial," Dan scoffed.

"Cut it out!" I said. "John can't control how long they stick around."

"Or how long *I* stick around," he quipped and made his escape.

It occurs to me that if John Edward heard that, he'd be an unhappy medium.

CHAPTER THREE - SEASONS READINGS

PARTYING IT UP ON NEW YEAR'S EVE

I REMEMBER FEELING restless that New Year's Eve. Up 'til then, I wondered what all the hoopla was about, but the year I turned thirteen, I *knew*. Parties...kissing...*Woooweee!* As I listened to Nancy Sinatra sing on my transistor radio, I longed to be part of the celebration. *Any* celebration. Instead, I was imprisoned at home with no tin cup to clang the bars.

Dozens of New Year's Eves have come and gone since then, many of which I saluted up close and personal. I anxiously awaited midnight, only to find my coach had turned into a pumpkin. Furthermore, after toasting the holiday at countless pubs and house parties, not one fiesta stands out in my memory. One *could* blame that on too much bubbly. But I've come to realize the revelry is overrated. In my humble opinion, there's no place like home to ring in the New Year.

That may or may not mean an evening with Dick Clark, the spiffy dude who never ages. I find it odd that I morphed from adolescence to middle age, while his looks stayed virtually the same. Or could it be each *New Year's Rockin' Eve* is merely a rerun from 1970?

Chances are we'll hear *Auld Lang Syne*, the song that never goes out of style—perhaps because it's so versatile. Sometimes bands jazz it up a bit or otherwise change the rhythm. Or some famous celebrity will sing the words while annihilating the tune. I have yet to hear it as a polka, but it's only a matter of time.

As a morning owl, my beef with New Year's Eve is that it lasts too long. To pass the time 'til midnight, here's a positive activity I read about. Write out twelve inspiring resolutions, roll them into scrolls and place them in a grab bag. Then each month select one and use it for kindling. Okay, that's not what the article said, but I like my idea better.

Then, as it's been since time began, the witching hour will usher in an impatient January, named for the Roman god, Janus. Like some people I know, he has two faces. In his case, one looks back at the year gone by and the other gazes forward to what lies ahead.

If it's all the same to him, I'd rather focus on the present.

BEFORE THE LAST SNOWFLAKE FALLS

IT REALLY BUGS me when folks start shoveling before it's stopped snowing. Like, is there some kind of status attached to that? I can just hear these people crow about it. "Hey, I beat all youse out here this morning!" Personally I don't head out until the last snowflake falls—even waiting a while to make sure no more white stuff trickles down. A day or two is usually sufficient.

I know it's time to act when I hear the drone of a snowblower off in the distance. Every once in a while our thoughtful neighbors, John and Jerry, steer their mighty machines down the sidewalk in front of our house. And every so often, Dan returns the favor with ours.

Like Tim Allen, he relishes a snowblower with loads of horsepower. Feeling the engine's brute force vibrating through his hands prompts him to go above and beyond the call of duty. One time he guided it down the block and out of sight. No telling how far he would have gone if some kid's misplaced toy hadn't locked up the auger.

Horsepower help is one thing. It's a little harder aiding neighbors with a lowly shovel. By the time I've finished, I'm too pooped to persevere. As it is, I stop every few yards to catch my breath and survey my progress. All the while, a little voice inside me asks, "Are we there yet?" Relief floods me when I line myself up with that imaginary property line. Not wanting to appear unneighborly, I shovel a few inches beyond that point and call it a day.

But on the way to the garage, I hear the #$%@ city snowplow behind me. I reel around in time to see a thick barrier form where I just shoveled. This happens too often to be mere coincidence.

To handle midwest snowfalls, one needs the right tool for the job. It's best to use a good, lightweight shovel. Ours, unfortunately, weighs a ton. We use it for barbells in the off season. It's okay for powdery, cold-weather snow, but I have an awful time with that tropical stuff. Wet, packy snow fuses itself to my scoop like static cling. Next time that happens, I'm gonna spray it with Pam and watch it slide right off.

And then *I'll* have something to crow about.

STILL COUNTING VALENTINES

IF THERE'S ONE thing I miss about grade school, it's valentines. Wearing rose-colored glasses, I eagerly tore open those dinky envelopes to giggle at silly one-liners and find out who really and truly loved me. In the afterglow, I counted each one and gathered them up for the happy trip home. It never once occurred to me that someone's mother probably signed them.

That fond memory tells me two things.

1. Perceived love is better than no love at all; and

2. A simple card means a lot.

Last year, an acquaintance itemized to me what her husband gave her for Valentine's Day. "I got flowers, a CD and some candy," she said, stifling a yawn.

"And what did you *really* want?" I asked.

"A cruise!" she replied without skipping a beat.

Maybe I'm missing something, but what that girl really needed (besides a kick in the butt) was a valentine. Not a store-bought, paid-in-installments sentiment, but one made by hand, using that heartwarming blend of construction paper and crayons.

Each year I read my son, Kelly, a book called *One Zillion Valentines* (Frank Modell, author) about a character named Marvin who teaches his pal, Milton, the true meaning of Valentine's Day. Together they make a wagonful of cards and deliver them to the neighborhood. Then they sell the leftovers and buy a box of chocolates to share.

Marvin knows valentines aren't just for lovers—they're for friends and neighbors, families and co-workers, and the guy who reads your meter. And handmade cards never fail to warm the heart. Even the homely cards.

At the risk of playing Pollyanna, I'd like to see everyone make a dozen simple greetings this holiday. Or buy those packaged valentines normally reserved for half pints. Then pass them out to those we encounter on a day-to-day basis—gas station clerks, prison guards, Tibetan monks...

Cards for out-of-towners would have to be mailed, of course, and the most cherished ones deserve a special postmark. Mail received by February 9th can be hand stamped with a "Loveland, Colorado" cachet and shipped off to your beloved. To accomplish this, send your pre-stamped, pre-addressed letters in a larger envelope to: Postmaster, ATTN: Valentines, USPS, Loveland, CO 80538-9998.

I may have aged a tad, but I'm still that romantic grade schooler at heart. I just need rose-colored bifocals now.

IDEAS FOR THE ROMANTICALLY CHALLENGED

NEED A STOCKING stuffer for Valentine's Day? Why not write your sweetheart a check for a million kisses? Or fill his or her car with red balloons? So suggests Gregory Godek, author of *1001 Ways to be Romantic*. One of *the* best relationship books of the century (in my humble opinion), I routinely present it as a wedding gift. Crystal may break and toasters may fry, but the goodwill gained from road testing *1001* can last forever.

Aimed at men and women of all ages and marital status, Godek's book encourages hiding love notes or little gifts where your partner is sure to find them. On his car seat...under her pillow...in his lunch box (so long as he acknowledges the contents before devouring them). Based on personal experience, however, I'd ignore his advice to tuck something 'in her purse' or it may never be seen again.

What *kind* of little gifts? Greeting cards, comic strips, tickets to movies or sporting events, her favorite candy bar, coupons for personal services... Anything that might bring a smile or out-and-out Snickers. (You *knew* I'd slide chocolate in there, didn't you?)

1001 includes hundreds of inexpensive ideas like taping his romantic horoscope to the bathroom mirror. Or making her a greeting card the size of the front door. And the greatest boon to romance requires no money whatsoever: stop nagging, complaining, correcting or lecturing your one-and-only. (Hey, nobody said this was easy.)

The book also contains suggestions that require some advance planning—like learning the guitar so you can play her a love song. Or saving the paper strips from a thousand Hershey kisses—then presenting them as coupons each good for a smooch. (*Note*: While I find this idea endearing, I'd *prefer* to receive the thousand Hershey kisses.)

Above all, Godek emphasizes the need for a positive frame-of-mind. "If you have the wrong mindset," he says, "you can turn a moonlit stroll on the beach into a fight."

Been there and done that. To illustrate the importance of an open mind, my sister met her husband when they were assigned to clean a utility room at the hospital. They fell in love amid the steamy setting of dirty bedpans. Nearly thirty years later, each day is *still* Valentine's Day for them.

For the rest of us, there's *1001*.

COUNTING ON CHOCOLATE

PERHAPS YOU'RE ONE of the million or so individuals to receive chocolates for Valentine's Day. If so, I hope your gift doesn't list nutrition facts like mine does. Eating a dozen treats loses its appeal when my sadistic brain keeps counting calories. And I'll thank it to stop tallying fat, too.

I appreciate the information set forth on Russell Stover candies, though. These days, the inside cover shows a detailed floor plan of the contents. Now I know right where to find my caramel clusters and can spot those putrid raspberry crèmes without poking my finger in them. I just hope my dysfunctional family doesn't rearrange them for kicks.

An aunt of mine who shall remain nameless said she opened a box of chocolates to find them somewhat grayish, a telltale sign that the shelf life had expired. Nevertheless, she tried one. Still unsure, she ate another. A handful more convinced her she should obtain a refund, but by the time she returned to the store, the second-rate sweets had vanished.

Homemade chocolates have a shorter life expectancy. I cooked up a big box of them for some friends of ours one year, but the holiday came and went without us socializing. Concerned that the treats might be stale, I tasted a few and put the rest in a smaller container. More time passed and, again, I sampled them for quality and transferred the remainder. Eventually I presented our pals with the gift. In a matchbox.

I decorated it pretty, though—almost as nice as those lavishly embellished heart-shaped boxes on the market. Have you noticed they get fancier each year? With their hundred yards of lace, they're virtual works of art. I can never bear to part with them, so I've stockpiled them in the attic. Right next to my Buns of Steel video.

Lace is fine and dandy but Chocomelt@aol.com (888-568-6665) sells boxes that are *made* of chocolate. Recipients eat the contents and then devour the container itself. That's my kind of recycling. And I like the idea of destroying the evidence, too.

That same company offers novelty chocolates shaped like full, sensuous lips as well as a twenty-five inch lady's leg with stocking and garter belt. I assume these are for guys. Chocolate or not, I'd feel uncomfortable nibbling on them.

So I'll stick with counting more conventional calories... 250...375...500...

THE WRITE TIME

ONE OF THE more thoughtful holidays to pop up in the last decade is Absolutely Incredible Kid Day. Launched five years ago and celebrated the third Thursday of March, it encourages adults, whether parents or not, to acknowledge special children in their lives by writing them a letter. And just where was this observance when *I* was an absolutely incredible kid?

Sour grapes aside, I think the better-late-than-never holiday is a fine idea—especially for those who put things like that off. When my son made his debut, I planned to write him periodic letters to record endearing moments and what his life has meant to me. But time disappeared faster than a paycheck.

Somehow I blinked and my newborn turned nine—halfway to that coveted (or dreaded, depending on viewpoint) age of freedom. I couldn't tell you where the years went. All I know is his jeans shrink a little more each week and our eyes are nearly level now. I hesitate to blink again for fear he'll fast forward to manhood.

So with peepers wide open I plan to participate in Absolutely Incredible Kid Day and urge readers to do the same. While there are no hard-and-fast rules, these guidelines may help:

1. Commit yourself to ten little minutes.
2. Cross outs are okay. Don't strive for perfection—no one's going to grade this.
3. It needn't be Michener-length. A page is more than enough to convey your message.
4. Remind him of a great memory you shared.
5. Congratulate her on a recent accomplishment.
6. Tell him what you like best about him.
7. Don't be afraid to be silly.
8. Don't be afraid to be mushy.
9. Sign it and seal it.
10. Mail it, email it, hide it in a backpack, or deliver it in person.

There's no time like the present to let kids know how we feel. *We* may be losing height, but they're sprouting up at a rapid rate. And our letters could warm their hearts long after we're gone.

But, hey, before we croak, let's establish an Absolutely Incredible *Adult* Day. And if you need my address, just lemme know.

UP TO MY NEW TRICKS

ONCE AGAIN, THANKS to my tireless efforts, I present my Annual List of April Fool's Jokes. These childish pranks are arranged chronologically so you can harass significant others, co-workers and the general public from sunrise to sunset. *Note*: The wise cracker plans an escape route before executing any of the following:

Painting The Clown Red: Polish your victim's fingernails (toenails, too, perhaps?) while he's sleeping.

Rise And Whine: Set an appliance timer to wake your stooge with a blaring stereo or TV.

Office Offense: Link your co-worker's paper clips together.

OJ...Innocent?: Fill small juice glasses with orange gelatin.

Thermos Be Some Mistake: Pour water into your target's thermos cap. Then turn thermos body upside down and screw onto the cap.

Vanishing Verbs: When your stooge steps away from her computer, change the font setting color to match the background.

When It Rains, It Floors: Fill your mark's umbrella with confetti and stand by for showers.

Post-It Prank: Post-It notes make this old classic a cinch to do. Write something profoundly amusing and attach it to your target's back side.

Please Pass The Volcano: You'll lava this messy joke! Empty a salt shaker and pour in lemon juice to about a third full. Cover opening with a tissue. Form an indent with your finger and add a teaspoon of baking soda. Screw the cover back on and snip off any excess tissue.

(Don't) Let Them Eat Cake: Cut two-inch-wide foam to standard cake size, 13 x 9". Frost and decorate as desired.

Do You Have This In A Larger Size?: Timing is everything, especially for this trick. Find yourself a strip of velcro or a rag that tears easily. Then place something of value on the floor and wait in the wings for your mark to pick it up. When he bends over, let 'er rip.

Audio Antics: Remove the gizmo from a musical greeting card and plant it some place your victim will make contact with—under his chair, in her purse, etc.

Romance Ruse: Place a looking-for-love ad in your target's name. If he's single, describe him contrary to his personality.

Pager Prank: Set off your favorite victim's beeper, leaving an April Fool's message. This is especially effective at bedtime.

And take the following steps to harass your favorite co-worker:

Use Super Glue (or its harmless cousin, Crazy Glue) to fasten 'loose' change to a vending machine's coin return and 'stick' around to witness the results. Then attach your victim's mouse to her mouse pad and watch her come unglued. Or dab a little under frequently used desk accessories.

Not her pencil holder though. If it's unbreakable, make use of this potentially entertaining item as follows: Push her office chair all the way in and tie fishing line to one of its legs. Wrap the other end around the pencil holder, which ideally is crammed with writing instruments. Then observe the action when your stooge enters her cubicle.

That is, if she's able. It may be difficult gaining access if you've filled it with balloons or crumpled up newspapers.

Or try the *Packing Peanuts Prank*. Cut a large opening in the bottom of a box. Fill it with packing peanuts and cover with a piece of cardboard. Then place it right side up on your victim's chair and remove the cardboard from underneath.

But wait—I've gotten ahead of myself! Before setting up any of the foregoing, you'll want to edit her computer program a bit. For a good time, take advantage of the AutoCorrect feature in Microsoft Word—the one that miraculously fixes our typos. To do this, click on Tools and AutoCorrect. In the Replace Box type a seldom-used word like 'the,' and in the With Box, type your *preferred* spelling (like 'da,' for instance).

Consider sabotaging these other areas as well:

Restroom: Leave an open bottle of lice powder on the counter, and pour some liquid dish detergent into the toilet tank.

Break Room: Release a sanitized rubber ducky in the water cooler, and mix some hot sauce in the ketchup dispenser.

And before your mark runs shrieking out the door, be sure to have this prank in place: Attach a wig to her car door with an oversized rubber band. Stretch it to reach under the seat and secure it with a clothespin. (Sorry, but I can't 'see' this one. What's supposed to happen?)

Tune in next year for practical jokes to play in the courtroom. When you're sued for harassment.

MANY UNHAPPY RETURNS

I HAVE TROUBLE doubling a recipe, so you can imagine how I feel about preparing a tax return. Nevertheless, each year I gather a flock of forms and my trusty calculator and set to work. Eight hours and half a bottle of Motrin later, I cross my fingers and mail it out.

But like my cookies, sometimes I omit a crucial ingredient. Last year I learned of a blooper when the refund arrived in the mail. In the accompanying notice, the IRS informed me that I goofed while ciphering a credit. As a result, the refund was far more generous than I'd figured.

That's good, of course—I could always use a new wardrobe.

It was the fine print that bothered me. Official Notice 54 went on to say that if I thought the check was too high, I should return it with a letter of explanation and they would lower it. What are they—*nuts!* What could possess me to give back a nice tidy sum like that? As a U.S. citizen, I know my rights under the Twenty-Eighth Amendment: finders-keepers.

The good news/bad news notice concluded with, "If you do not return the check, you may owe interest." In other words, I get charged extra if the IRS messed up.

And it certainly *could* mess up. According to District Director Steve Jensen, mistakes occur "twenty percent of the time." That's a lot of unhappy returns. And they aren't necessarily little booboos either. In one case, the IRS inadvertently raised someone's adjusted gross income from $4,668 to $446,800. It took a year of high anxiety to straighten things out.

Most errors occur when clerks input a return's data into the computer. To avoid this, taxpayers are encouraged to file electronically. My guess is they are less likely to hold down the zero key.

But how do I sign an electronic return? I wondered, so I spent two days researching the quickie way to file. The answer lies on a PIN. (That must hurt.) People choose any random five-digit personal identification number to use for their signature. As usual, not everyone qualifies. Deceased taxpayers cannot obtain a PIN and must file the old-fashioned way.

Besides an increase in accuracy, electronic filing enables us to get our refund check faster. That way we can fight over what to spend it on sooner.

THE HISTORY OF MUMMY'S DAY

DON'T FORGET (AS if you could) that Mother's Day is right around the calendar. But there's still time to buy cards, candy or a Cadillac for Mom, Mama, or the more formal Mother. Whatever her handle, she's the one person who unconditionally loves you despite your obnoxious faults.

It all started back in 1908 when Anna Reeves Jarvis held the first celebration of motherhood. There ensued a relentless campaign to make it an annual event. Five years later, the U.S. Congress officially founded Mother's Day. And we've been finding it ever since.

President Woodrow Wilson proclaimed it a national holiday in 1914. Of course, folks didn't have TVs back then to remind them during commercial breaks about that second Sunday of May. They had to rely on jumbo newspaper ads to hammer it into their heads. Luckily, Hallmark had already debuted, so thousands of people could send the same highly personal greeting to their mummy.

Human nature being what it is, it didn't take long for commercialism to cloak the holiday. This upset Anna Reeves Jarvis who, just before dying, said she was sorry she had ever started Mother's Day. It probably didn't help matters that she never had kids. No well-meaning child ever served her a breakfast in bed of scrambled eggshells. No wonder she was bitter!

After seeing an ad urging me to buy Mother a jacuzzi, I agree with Anna that things have gotten a little out of hand. Sure, moms deserve to be pampered, but we shouldn't have to mug Bill Gates to finance it. There are plenty of other ways to show our gratitude for bringing us into this greedy, violent, deceitful world. (Hey, she *meant* well.)

The most treasured gift we can give Mom is our time. Spend an afternoon together reminiscing about the dumb things you did as a child. Or the even dumber thing you did the other day.

Make her a card. Because you care *more than* enough to send a store-bought one.

Give her a certificate for some service. Better yet, a whole coupon book like that sticky one you made in grade school.

Cook her favorite meal, but don't leave her sink full of dishes this time.

Suggest a game of cards or her favorite amusement. No cheating.

Give her a 100% genuine, satisfaction-or-your-money-back hug.

Or take her for a nice walk—but steer clear of that Cadillac dealership.

"M" IS FOR...

I DON'T REFER TO my mom as Mother so I penned new lyrics to that famous tune written a few years back (songwriter unknown). With all due respect to the original version, mine more aptly honors the lady I've always called Mumma.

"M" is for possessing *Mucho* patience...

Like the time she found a dead bird my brother, Jim, had stashed under his bed. It was never clear if he saved it for burial or dissection purposes, but suffice it to say, he'd stored it too long.

As I recall, the only time she *lacked* patience was waiting for her dandelion wine to ferment...

"U" means *Understanding* through and through...

That's better than that line about growing old, isn't it? Besides, I wouldn't insult Mumma's age—my sister did that enough when we were teens. Chatting about a forty-some-year-old woman one day, Joan blurted out, "She's really *old*, Mom—she's as old as you!"

Mumma was understanding when it came to *my* bloopers, too. Lost in a department store at the tender age of four, I described her to a nearby clerk. "She has mousy brown hair and red lips," I said between sobs. She still jokes about us tracking her down based on that description...

"M" is for the many things you *Made* me...

Like the dresses she whipped up for my sister and me—matching numbers of chiffon and lace that were so poufy we had to walk single file.

Or the Christmas she wrapped up a huge box of Barbie doll clothes she'd sewn. As my eight-year-old eyes feasted on a rainbow of shimmering gowns and elegant fur stoles, I thought I'd died and gone to Barbie Paris.

"M" is for fond *Memories* of you...

Like the time she cleverly hid Jim's Easter treat in a basket of dirty laundry. But Sherlock found it anyway.

Or the year she took part in a cookie exchange, but cheated and bought hers from a bakery.

"A" is for your numerous *Achievements*...

Blind to all but those who care to see...

For years she ran a full-time business, while maintaining an impeccable house. And *still* she had the wherewithal to nurture a family as crazy as ours.

Put them all together—they spell Mumma.

You bet she means the world to me.

SAVED BY MY VIRTUAL MODEL

IT'S ALMOST SWIMSUIT Season—a term that strikes fear in the hearts of figure-conscious women. Normally I would launch a desperation diet right about now, but this year I adopted a different strategy—finding a suit that fits me rather than the other way around.

That's harder than it sounds. My shape inspires four different sizes: one from a wannabe bust, one from runaway hips, and two from a waistline that ebbs and flows, depending on the time of day. In my search, I've learned the best suit for my melting pot of measurements is the tankini. Dissected, that's "tank" as in tank top and "kini" as in two pieces that don't play tug o' war like opposite ends of a one-piece do.

Lands' End sent me a catalog swimming with tankinis this year, each modeled by women who appear well adjusted despite being severely malnourished. It's one of several companies now offering a service called My Virtual Model (www.myvirtualmodel.com). Those with Internet access can build a model using their very own personal data and let *her* do the grunt work.

This sounded like a painless way to shop, so I gave it a try. After divulging my name, rank and measurements, a virtual model appeared on my screen. Besides sharing my height and shape, she mirrored my hairstyle and skin tone—minus wrinkles, of course. And she already sported a casual outfit from Lands' End. I hate to sound catty, but it did *nothing* for her. So I urged her into the swimsuit department where she swiftly donned a dozen styles, one after another. She modeled tankinis, "slender suits" and even full-length cover-ups but, frankly, they all looked better on the hanger.

Despite the frustrating ordeal, her mood never changed. She didn't cuss out the manufacturer for its faulty sizing. And she didn't slump into a dressing room chair crying, "Why am I so fat?" She just held her head up and kept right on smiling.

That impressed me to no end. And even though I failed to make a purchase, I came away from my cyber shopping trip with a positive feeling. If My Virtual Model can maintain her cool, then so can I! So this weekend I'm headed for the local shops.

I just hope they have a mannequin in my size.

THE *IM*PERFECT WEDDING

WHEN IT COMES to weddings, people tend to get caught up in perfection. If you saw the ill-fated show, *Who Wants to Marry a Millionaire?*, you know what a flawless event it highlighted. Millions of viewers watched as a perfect looking girl married a perfectly loaded guy.

The same goes for run-of-the-mill nuptials. The moment the happy couple gets engaged, the emphasis immediately turns to planning the 'perfect wedding.' I get a kick out of brides-to-be who spare no expense in their pursuit. Cinderella gowns, cakes that require scaffolding, and don't forget the horse-drawn carriage!

Furthermore, the parties must act as flawless as they look. No occasion screams for etiquette like getting hitched. A pack of picky protocol books is available to ensure everything is done according to

Hoyle (or, more accurately, Miss Manners). I checked one out to see what's proper and what's not these days. It featured an easy question-and-answer format for inquiring but etiquette-impaired minds.

Typical queries included, "Is there a wrong way to cut wedding cake?" (with a chainsaw) and "Is it ever too late to send thank-you notes?" (after signing the divorce judgment). One question I didn't expect to see was, "Can the hostess ask the caterer to wrap up all the leftovers?" To my great amazement, the author said this is perfectly acceptable. Why didn't someone *tell* me I could have a doggy bag?

Chances are, the happy couple registered at some hoidy-toidy department store, so the house they set up will be perfect, too. After the reception, they'll eagerly tear open those perfectly wrapped gifts despite already knowing what's in them.

And after the last crystal goblets have been forced out of hiding, what then? Why, the perfect honeymoon, of course! Maybe they'll take a romantic love boat cruise or spend a luxuriating week in Maui. No need to leave the light on, Motel 6. This'll be first class all the way.

I feel sorry for these folks. After basking in all that perfection, it'll be tough coming back to the real world. And paying that charge card off is no picnic either.

But, hopefully, they'll settle down into a happy (and perfect) relationship, unlike the couple on *Who Wants to Marry a Millionaire?* Their marriage lasted a mere twenty-four days before Darva Conger filed for an annulment from Rick Rockwell.

But, then again, they were 'perfect' strangers.

A TIMELY TOAST

HAVE YOU NOTICED some wedding toasts last longer than the unions they salute? It seems folks just don't know when to quit yakking or the proper thing to say for the occasion. With the nuptial season upon us, I thought it fitting to set forth a few basic rules for toasting the bride and groom.

1. Does this place look like Gettysburg? You can have the floor for two minutes or two hundred words, whichever comes first. After that we want it back.

2. To keep it brief; omit quirky words such as 'like.' For instance, "I first, like, met the bride when she, like, made a pass at me." This not only drags out the toast but is aggravating to people who don't like 'like.' Likewise, don't abuse 'okay,'

okay?

3. See that couple who look like they jumped off a cake top? Keep them in mind when you tell your amusing anecdote. This is *their* day and guests want to hear about *them*, not your sorry life.

4. Refrain from using big words, unless you're handing out complementary dictionaries.

5. One word: sincerity. No need to ramble about the bride and groom's eternal love for each other. Trust me, they'll run into the same problems as the rest of us.

6. If you don't have access to a microphone, speak loudly enough we can hear you in the back, but, *Hey, no need to shout*!

7. If a mike *is* available, don't use the opportunity to launch a singing career. Do us all a favor and save it for karaoke night.

8. Speak clearly. Thish ish no time to shlur your wordj. Sure, you wanna celebrate, but wait 'til after your little speech to get polluted. And in the same vein, toast the happy couple before you refill your plate ten times. Your delivery is much more effective without gas.

9. Practice, practice, practice.

10. Strive for originality. That touching toast may be new to you, but chances are, the rest of us fossils heard it a dozen times before. If you can't conjure up your own tribute, feel free to use this one with my blessing:

The bride pursued, a groom she got—
Two aces make a deuce.
Let's toast the pair who tied the knot,
And hope it ain't a noose.

THE PERFECT PRESENT FOR POP

WITH FATHER'S DAY approaching, I'm faced with the question of what to buy the dad who has everything. Ties are out. He owns dozens, but I've yet to see him wear one with his favorite sweatshirt. And who wants to give hankies, knowing *their* sorry fate?

No—the gift should be something thoughtful that reflects Pop's personality. As a kid, Dad's favorite prank was to plant stink bombs and spy at a distance to see the results. Sixty years haven't dimmed his taste for practical jokes, so maybe I should giftwrap a whoopee cushion.

At age eleven, Dad became fascinated with cameras, a hobby that eventually led to his own photography business. Consequently, he's snapped a few pictures during his lifetime, so perhaps he could use a photo album. A really thick one.

Thanks to army duty in Tokyo, Dad learned how to say, "It hurts," and count to twenty in Japanese. That's fine if he stubs a toe or needs to calm down, but what about eating? Suppose he has to order a meal or something? So maybe a foreign language tape is in order.

Before we rugrats arrived, Dad tuned in to *The Shadow* and other programs for entertainment. I'd buy him a new radio if I thought it could compete with HBO.

My favorite memories include playing duets with Pop at the piano. One of us usually messed up in the middle and we'd stumble through the rest of the tune. I could give him a CD so we could hear how the songs *should* have sounded.

Dad served as resident driver's ed instructor, bravely accompanying us on our practice runs. Then he bought a second vehicle so we'd have our own wheels (or maybe so *he'd* have *his*?). So a thoughtful gift, in lieu of a car, might be an honorary teaching certificate.

I warmly recall backyard barbecues with Dad as head chef. He wielded a mean spatula in his quest for char-broiled burgers. In honor of that memory, I should present him with a fire extinguisher.

In recent years, Dad has turned his attention to computers. Starting on a Tandy-asaurus, he worked his way up to a Pentium 4. I could buy him another PC, but he already has a basement full.

So what's the perfect present for Pop?

Only the Shadow knows.

HUGS, NOT SHRUGS

MY EIGHT-YEAR-OLD SON doesn't dole out hugs as freely as he once did. Not only are they less frequent, but they're brief as heck. When I embrace him a second too long, he shrugs away like a cat from Pepe LePew.

As a touchy-feely person, I find this development hard to swallow. To paraphrase Dr. David Bresler, it takes four hugs a day to survive, eight to maintain, and twelve to grow. I could see that quota and raise a few.

Hugs are so therapeutic. They have a way of making good times great and troubling times not so bad. They bring people closer. And you can execute them in any number of ways.

First, there's the face-to-face method. Of course, each party eventually turns his or her head to avoid embarrassment. However, it's hard dodging someone's face if you rotate in the same direction. I'd like to see Miss Manners establish some etiquette so we'd know which way to turn.

Some people add a few pats on the back for good measure. This is my dad's trademark. In fact, he's still patting long after the embrace is over. If done properly, this type of hug generates feelings of warmth and security as well as a fairly decent burp.

In a bear hug, the larger person generally wraps his arms around the smaller one's shoulders. Technically, this could last as long as the big guy desires, but a good rule of claw is five seconds.

The back-to-front hug often takes the huggee by surprise. Depending on the hugger's height, she can gently squeeze the other person's shoulders, waist or ankles.

Any of these two-party methods can be combined with the rocking hug, which is a gentle motion like a boat swaying in waves. *Note*: Prolonged exposure may cause seasickness.

But hugs aren't limited to two people. Every so often, we call for a family hug. Also known as the sandwich hug, this consists of two outer layers (my husband and me) with 'Kelly filling' in between.

And group hugs can consist of any number of consenting persons. We must remember, however, that not everyone enjoys close contact. Embracing these folks is like hugging a wooden soldier. So for their sake (and yours), hands off.

But the rest of us can look forward to World Hug Week in July. And try our darnedest to reach that quota.

A GARLIC GROUPIE?

MY BETTER HALF whips up his own relish now. He measures a titch of this and a tad of that and blends it 'til it resembles phlegm. One might say it's the spittin' image. Then he spreads it on anything that can't outrun him.

I don't partake in this delicacy and wouldn't mention it if it didn't directly affect me. But since this condiment kick started, I've been assaulted on a daily basis by the main ingredient.

You know how I hate to complain, but few things smell worse than second hand garlic. No wonder vampires avoid it. The aroma ranks right up there with aged gym clothes. To make matters worse, garlic connoisseurs have the ability to project their breath over a five-mile radius.

It all started when Dan learned about its medicinal benefits. Studies show garlic lowers cholesterol levels as well as blood pressure. The heart smart plant also improves circulation. Furthermore, and this was news to me, it's believed to have an effect on impotence, although no one can get close enough to say for sure.

With all of that going for it, Dan now applies garlic powder with a heavy hand, not only to his world famous relish, but everything else he devours. It's only a matter of time before he becomes a Gilroy Garlic Festival groupie. The annual event takes place in California the last full weekend of July. (For information, call 408-842-1625.)

I'll give you three guesses what flavor rules at the popular celebration. Last year, roughly a hundred and twenty thousand folks attended, each somehow oblivious to the others' horrific breath. Highlights of the fragrant fiesta include the Great Garlic Cook-Off, which nets the lucky winner a thousand bucks and a crown of garlic. And those so inclined can shake their booty at the Garlic Squeeze Barn Dance, where I assume they leave the doors open.

But perhaps the most significant event—at least to the contestants—is the crowning of Miss Gilroy Garlic. The 'Belle of the Bulb' is judged in talent and evening gown competitions and a 'garlic speech.' Words are all well and good, but actions speak volumes. I say the winner should be whomever scores highest on a breathalyzer test.

Meanwhile back at the ranch, I'm learning to cook with garlic, safe in the knowledge that it remedies all kinds of conditions. I have only one question.

What's the cure for garlic breath?

NOTHING BUT GNATS

I WATCHED A FRAIL, elderly man carry a tennis racket to the checkout counter. With trembling hands, he pulled out his wallet and paid the clerk. Too curious to mind my own business, I asked, "Are *you* gonna play tennis?"

"No," he grumbled. "I have a bat in my basement."

Besides a chuckle, the encounter prompted a flood of memories. Years ago, a school chum and I played tennis—not because we liked it, but because the objects of our desire hung out at the court. And we swooned and batted our eyes each time they called out 'seven—love.'

I was never what you'd call athletically inclined and, after reaching adulthood (though that's up for debate), I left the arena completely. But this year I've made an effort to join the sporting life. My son, his grandpa and I play basketball quite often now. Nothing too regimented, of course—just lots of free throws culminating in a game of Clydesdale. (That's like Horse only it lasts longer.)

"Hey!" I yelled one day. "The ball's outta bounce!"

"That's supposed to be 'bounds,' Mom."

"No, this thing's got a leak in it," I said, plucking it off the cement.

We discovered the joy of frisbee throwing, too. With a fair amount of practice, one can send it right where one aims: in a tree...on the roof...under the car...and—on rare occasions—to the intended receiver. "I threw that one so good you couldn't catch it!" Kelly yelled one time, as I chased down another fugitive.

I like it best when the flying saucer sails merrily through the air. The game loses its fun when it bears down on its target like a scud missile. In that case, I either scream and cover my head or accept the challenge and let my defenseless hand take a beating. Like tennis elbow and runner's knee, there oughta be a name for injuries like that. Maybe they should call it frisbee fingers.

Less violent, but every bit as frustrating, is badminton. That's because it takes longer to set up the net than it does to play. Furthermore, the little birdie is at the mercy of the wind, and when the gale dies down, players are hounded by a horde of gnats. But a good racket, when used properly, helps fend off airborne intruders.

I learned that tip from a fellow consumer.

MADE IN THE SHADES

ONE MIGHT CONCLUDE from my collection of useless sunglasses that I have trouble buying them. And one would be right. This is because I feel silly trying them on. The mirrors on the display racks don't conform to my eye-level so I have to stand on tippy-toes to see. Then I throw in a casual pose or two to get the full effect.

By this time, a half-dozen shoppers have stopped to witness my peculiar antics. Hey, this isn't a spectator sport, folks! I wish stores would install dressing rooms so we serious sunglass buyers could do our thing in peace.

Peepers are important. We must protect them from the damaging effects of the sun. The question you should ask your friendly neighborhood dealer is, "Will these sunglasses block a hundred percent of the sun's UVA rays?" Not, "Do you have any that make me look like a Blues Brother?"

Besides shielding our eyes and morphing your Average Joe into Joe Cool, sunglasses serve an additional purpose. They hide tears. I'm a frequent crier and appreciate the chance to cover up after a good bawl. It's harder to see the movie, though.

As a blue-eyed former blonde (as well as an assortment of other dyes), my eyes are especially sensitive to the light. I've spent a lifetime squinting and had crow's feet by age five. You'd think I'd possess some decent sunglasses by now. But, despite having a gaggle of goggles, I still don't have it made in the shades.

One pair I own has some type of blue coating on them. They cut the glare and lent me a rather snazzy appearance when new. But after tumbling around in my purse a few months, they look like Captain Hook cleaned them.

The lenses pop out of another pair I own. And still another sits cockeyed on my nose. If I had a favorite, it would be my mirrored ones because they give the short-lived impression I'm chic. But they don't fit well and surrender to gravity when I look down. It's hard acting vogue when your glasses dive off your face.

Imagine that happening to Stevie Wonder! And how does he keep tabs on his eyewear anyway? The few decent pairs I've bought have vanished within days. But for some reason my dysfunctional shades hang around forever.

Hence my sorry collection.

FAIR TO MIDWAY

MY VIEW OF THE local fair has evolved over the years. As a kid, it meant blowing my allowance on umpteen games of darts and spinning on the Tilt-A-Whirl 'til I tossed my cotton candy.

My romantic teen years saw me yearning to ride the Ferris wheel with heartthrob David Cassidy. As an adult, I thrilled over winning a ribbon for my chocolate chip cookies. But now I'm a parent, the fair means pawning our house to finance the annual trip.

The cheapest route is to buy an armband for an afternoon of all-you-can-ride. Children wear the twelve-dollar investment around their wrist and parents threaten them with amputation if they remove it. Then the munchkins can spin and slide and squeal into infinity or 'til they get bored, whichever comes first.

With nothing else to do, parents absently memorize the warning sign that accompanies each ride. It cautions guests to expect "strong back to back forces, rapidly changing heights and strong side to side forces." Somehow I find it hard to believe that Choo Choo Charlie, a train traveling six inches an hour, could cause that kind of turbulence. The notice further alerts people not to ride under the influence of drugs, so I guess all those kids on Ritalin are outta luck.

We learned from experience to eat *after* the rides. When the Twister has lost its twinkle, we mosey down the midway to find our favorite food vendor. There we share a plate of tempura, a savory mix of veggies dipped in batter and deep-fried to a golden brown. At least I *think* they're veggies. Truth is, I'd eat sod if they fixed it like that. For dessert, we down wedges of ice cream dipped in chocolate and sprinkled with nuts. They appear to have shrunk a bit since I was a kid, or maybe my eyes got bigger. In any case, they're still yummy as ever.

We usually amble over to the arcade tent, too. There, Kelly plays a few rounds of pinball with whatever change I have left while I try hard to keep from melting. Someday they'll charge a sauna fee at the door.

When every last cent is gone, it's time to leave.

"Did you have fun?" I ask my Number One Son.

"Yup!" he replies. "How 'bout you?"

"Oh...fair to midway."

GIVE A MAN A FISHY...

GIVE A MAN A FISH and you feed him for a day. Teach a man to fish and I swear that's all he thinks about.

My husband Dan lives for those quiet, reflective moments when he trolls the bay soaking up nature 'til he tires of swatting it. When he's not fishing, anticipating fishing or coming back from fishing, he's reading fishing magazines. And you should see the centerfolds.

Dan likes to *talk* about his hobby, too. I get a blow-by-blow account of each voyage, complete with well-worn excuses.

"How'd it go?" I ask, though I can plainly see he's empty-handed.

"It was too (insert one: windy, rough, cold, etc.)..." Like the Three Bears, conditions are never quite right. Then he describes the huge, enormous, colossal, Holy-wah-ya-should've-*Seen*-it! fish that got away.

Every so often Dan feels the need to defend his obsession. "Look how much we save on our food bill," he tells me.

"But...don't you have to catch a fish to do that?" I ask, feigning innocence.

The other day he actually reeled one in and boasted about his 'free lunch.'

I pointed out that if you add up the cost of the pole and the annual license, not to *mention* the boat, his meal was far from gratuitous. He dismissed those expenses as an 'initial investment.'

"Okay. Then what about tackle?" I said, clearly on a roll. "You've got box full and *still* you belong to the Lure of the Month Club."

Dan gave me 'the look' and explained to his addled wife, "Different types of tackle attract different fish."

I should have quit while I was behind, but instead I persisted. "Why don't you just use night crawlers? *All* fishies like them, don't they?"

"They cost too much," he replied. "I had to fork out a couple dollars for a dozen the other day."

"You paid *two bucks* for worms? Why...you could buy a fish sandwich *already cooked* for that price!"

I could see where things were headed, so I calmed myself down. "Tell ya what," I said. "Next time you buy night crawlers, save two."

"Excuse me?"

"That way you can breed 'em," I reasoned. "And the profits can support your fishing habit."

DON'T TRY THIS AT HOMESCHOOL

I RAN INTO ONE of my son's former classmates the other day. "How come Kelly's not in school this year?" she asked.

"He's homeschooled," I said. "How would *you* like to do that?"

"No way!" she replied. "I get *three* recesses!"

In her curious way, she confirmed what I already knew: it's not for everyone. Homeschooling requires a major commitment, both in actual teaching and behind-the-scenes operations. And patience is a virtue that escapes me at times. I marvel at teachers who manage whole classrooms without Valium.

The good news is parent-teacher conferences are a breeze. I just talk to myself. And should we continue to the normal conclusion, my son would graduate at the top of his class.

Seriously, I enjoy the sense of accomplishment that comes from teaching Kelly. And one of the fringe benefits of homeschooling is that parents re-learn facts they thought they'd never forget. I've been humbled more than once by a book called *What Your Third Grader Needs to Know.* (E.D. Hirsch)

Although homeschoolers are a pretty diverse bunch, most have one thing in common. We tend to go overboard buying curriculum. This year I bought my eight-year-old a college algebra book and three foreign language courses. And while my husband, Dan, takes it all in stride, he did question me on one purchase. "Lemme get this straight—you paid $18.95 for a book called *Homeschool Your Child for Free?*" (LauraMaery Gold)

Despite its growing popularity, many still view homeschooling as a radical concept. Even our computer's spell checker rejects the word, suggesting 'homicide' instead. Frankly, it's crossed my mind...

...especially when some Bozo brings up socialization. Honestly, folks, we don't lock our kid in a closet. Whereas Kelly once was timid, he now yaks it up with anyone in earshot. He belongs to several organizations and has friends up the kazoo. I should be so lucky as to have his social life.

Homeschooling is as much a lifestyle as it is an educational choice. It's hard at times to shut down from teacher mode, and the least little thing can launch it again—like the time I opened a pop bottle. "Can you name the gas that just escaped?" I quizzed Kelly.

"Methane," he said with a chuckle that swelled into a full guffaw.

Just for the record, he didn't learn that from me.

A FEMININE ATHLETIC SUPPORTER

NEITHER RAIN NOR sleet nor Monday night can keep me from seeing the Packers play this year. For the first time since my eight-year-old was born, I watch football without interruptions. While he putters on his 'puter and Dan tinkers with his truck, I don a tacky green-and-gold wardrobe and park myself in front of the tube.

Granted, this is quite a role reversal. In most households, the guys make like couch potatoes and shout, "Hey, honey—could ya bring me a beer?" But in *this* huddle, I'm the official athletic supporter.

Unfortunately, my attention span isn't very long. Though my adrenaline flows like crazy during kickoff, it loses momentum by the third quarter. Just guessing here, but I bet the players feel the same way. Furthermore, I only like watching when *my* team has the ball. When the defensive unit hits the field, I generally hit the fridge.

True, I could miss a crucial interception, but that's the beauty of instant replay. Should anything remotely exciting occur, it'll be repeated from a hundred different angles. Makes me wonder where all the camera guys are and why they never get tackled.

I wouldn't dream of leaving during commercials which, depending on my team's savvy, may be the only thing worth watching. For some reason, sponsors save their most entertaining ads for football games as though only predominantly male viewers have a sense of humor. Don't they know women gag over those stain-remover testimonials found on daytime TV? Like, get with the program!

That aside, I stretch out on the couch spouting original slogans like, "Go, team, Go!" and hoot over ads. But truth is, being the only groupie in the house gets kind of lonely. A cheering section of one doesn't have the same effect as a roomful of rabid fans. I feel downright silly hollering when my team scores. And when it screws up, there's no one to take it out on except my frustration doll.

So when halftime comes, I seek out my family. "Wanna finish the game with me?" I ask Dan the Man. A grunt tells me he's busy so I wander over to my son. "Hey, let's watch the game together!" I shout, as though the idea just occurred to me.

"No thanks, Mom," he replies.

Then I wander back to the couch to finish my uninterrupted game.

SPILLING THE BEANS

AS AN AMERICAN, I'm grateful to Christopher Columbus for discovering what many of us citizens would die for. Chocolate.

Forget that prove-the-earth-is-round theory! The guy's real motive was to satisfy his sweet tooth. Cocoa beans were among the exotic treasures he found in the New World, and he returned to his native land with a mouth-watering cartful.

For those scientific types out there, cocoa beans come from the Theobroma cacao tree. Cacao is how cocoa looks before proofreading. And Theobroma means food of the gods, who I'm fairly certain had a weight problem. The Aztec Indians made a drink from the beans, which Emperor Montezuma supposedly downed fifty times a day. And you can guaran-damn-tee it wasn't Slim Fast.

Aware of its value, the Aztecs used cocoa beans for money. For example, five beans might purchase a Rolex. With today's inflation, the same watch would cost fifty beans and a Kit Kat bar.

For nearly a century, Spain processed its cacao in monasteries under a veil of secrecy. As you may know, monks don't engage in idle chitchat and neither do they play charades. But, luckily for the rest of us, someone eventually spilled the beans.

Cocoa's all well and good, but my personal favorite, solid chocolate, didn't come along until 1847. Both products start out the same way. The beans must first be sorted, roasted and winnowed. For those unfamiliar with the term, that means their husbands died. And I dedicate every candy bar I eat to their memory.

People are quick to criticize my favorite flavor. "It causes cavities," they say. Or "It raises cholesterol levels." Picky, picky, picky! The good news is a study by the U.S. Naval Academy revealed chocolate does *not* cause acne. What some people won't do for the sake of research.

Some day I hope to tour a chocolate factory from whence sweet things emerge (with the exception of Jeffrey Dahmer). If the thrill proves too much for my ticker, at least I'll die happy. And they can bury me in a giant Easter Bunny mold.

In the meantime, I celebrate National Chocolate Day on October 28. That's when I fill my cart with swarms of Snickers bars and mobs of Milky Ways. "I get lots of trick-or-treaters," I tell the cashier, suppressing hysterical laughter. So far she hasn't suspected a thing.

I got that line from Columbus.

THERE SHE ISN'T

THERE THEY ARE...the Miss America contestants! Folks so inclined have the thrill of watching the eighty-something annual pageant in October. Lucky skudders.

To make the event more fulfilling, viewers are urged to call 1-800-360-2312 and order this year's pageant program book. The informative keepsake offers photos and biographical sketches of each contestant. Those hawking it say it's sure to be a collector's item. Yeah, right. Tell that to the fifty losers who tear it to shreds.

A while back, I suggested the presidential election might benefit from imitating beauty pageants—a swimsuit competition to liven up debates, etc. That was just plain nonsense. But I could see the Miss America Pageant copying the election process. Why should that crucial decision be left to a panel of judges who never pick the right girl? I say we head to the polls and do it the democratic way.

Elections tend to bring out the worst in people, though. I can just hear the candidates engage in mudslinging.

"Miss Congeniality had a boob job!"

And Miss Con might counter with, "Oh, yeah? Well, *she* slept with the emcee !"

Contestants are judged by the following criteria: Talent, forty percent ; Interview, thirty percent ; On-stage Personality in Evening Wear, fifteen percent ; and Physical Fitness in Swimsuit, fifteen percent. In the event of a tie, the candidate who can add those percentages correctly is the winner.

The qualifications for becoming Miss A have certainly evolved over the years. 'Wholesome' best describes prior years' contestants, who were barely allowed to have cavities. Although today's hopefuls must still be single and childless, they can now be divorced and/or the recipient of an abortion. In the pageant board's efforts to avoid discrimination laws, wholesomegot a bit tarnished.

Well, what about that discriminating age rule? Frankly, I'd like to see it changed to allow older, more mature types like me to enter. After all, we're American women, too! Anyone regardless of age should be eligible, provided they can hobble up that runway. But, no. That would discriminate against paraplegics. Better idea—construct wheelchair ramps and then *no one* would be excluded.

Except men, of course. But any day now, some guy will sue the pageant board for discrimination and then everyone, regardless of gender, will be vying for the title of Miss America. They'd have to change the theme song though. How about *There He Is...*? Or maybe, *There She Isn't..."*

THE TRICK OR TREAT BEAT

I STILL RECALL THE thrill of trick or treating at night. Dressed incognito, my sister and I would steal up to each house cloaked in darkness. Convening back at the sidewalk, we'd pass judgment on the candy dispensed. ("Peanut butter kisses? Yech!")

·   Then we'd peer in our sacks under streetlights to see how much loot we'd amassed. Somehow it never looked like much 'til we got home and dumped it on the floor. I'm not sure how many miles my brother put on his runners, but he'd roll in sometime after midnight dragging a fifty-pound treat bag.

Times have changed since then. For safety purposes, trick or treat now takes place in broad daylight and lasts two hours. Good idea, yes, but that feeling of adventure got lost in the shuffle.

There aren't as many people home at that time of day either. Often only a house or two per block participates, which means a lot of legwork for my Number One Son. Then again, he'd walk a mile for a caramel.

Kelly covers the same beat his mom did thirty-odd years ago. Only the names have changed. And like his old lady, he returns home breathless from his travels. Then he sits at the table and sorts his collection into three neat piles—one for chocolate, one for hard candy, and a third for razor blades.

Meanwhile, I hand out candy to hordes of action figures from the latest blockbuster movie. And while they may dress alike, they come in all shapes and sizes. Some trick-or-treaters are so young, they can't remember their lines. They scale our porch like Mount Everest and greet me with a wide-eyed look, assuming I know what to do.

Others travel in gangs that tower over me. They generally show up just before this annual free-for-all ends. "Aren't you guys a little old?" I ask as I dispense the treats. Shaquille, the head spokesperson, voices a clever retort, and the group trots off to the next supplier.

That is, assuming I have any candy left. No matter how much I buy, I run out before the last vampire visits. All that's left in the bowl are empty wrappers and no one seems to want them.

Perhaps I should start buying peanut butter kisses.

CALL OF THE RILED

OPERATOR: YOU'VE REACHED 9-1-1. Go ahead.

Me: I need (cough) help right away. This is (cough) an emergency!

Operator: Try to stay calm, ma'am. Tell me where you are and your current situation.

Me: I'm (cough) in the kitchen and it's full of (cough) smoke.

Operator: Okay, listen carefully. I want you to drop to the floor and crawl outside.

Me: Wouldn't it be (cough) easier just to open a window? That's what I (cough) usually do.

Operator: This has happened before?

Me: Every year, just like (cough) clockwork.

Operator: Hmmmm...well, I've been trained in situations like this and know the best way to proceed. As I said before, I want you to crawl out of the house.

Me: (cough) No.

Operator: What d'ya mean, "No"?

Me: Who'd finish cooking dinner if I (cough) left?

Operator: Now listen here, ma'am. I can't save your life if you won't cooperate.

Me: Gosh, (cough) lady! That's not why I (cough) called. I just wanna know how to (cough) make gravy.

Operator: (sigh) Have you ever considered the Butterball hotline, ma'am?

Me: Ain't that who I'm talkin' to? It's hard to see the phone buttons in all this smoke.

Click

Operator: You've reached the Butterball hotline. How may I help you?

Me: Well, it's about time! I've been on hold for an hour. Darn turkey's so cold it turned up the thermostat.

Operator: Sorry, ma'am. We're pretty busy this time of year.

Me: How busy are ya?

Operator: We receive a hundred and seventy thousand callers each season.

Me: Well, here's your hundred-seventy-thousand-*first*, so listen up. How do I make gravy?

Operator: First, remove your poultry from the pan.

Me: Already gave my husband the bird. What's next?

Operator: Leave the crusty stuff in the pan for flavor.

Me: No problem—it's been stuck to it for years.

Operator: Now pour your drippings into a bowl and skim off your fat.

Me: Mine or the turkey's?

Operator: Return a quarter cup of fat to the pan and add a quarter cup of flour. Cook and stir over medium heat 'til bubbly.

Me: You mean like that goofy aerobics instructor I once had?

Operator: Add enough water or broth to your drippings to equal two cups of liquid. Now pour into the pan and cook and stir 'til thick.

Me: Hey, it turned out! Thanks a lot, Betty!

Operator: Betty?

Me: Crocker. Get it?

Click

HARK! THE LITTLE DARLINGS SING!

I SAW IT ADVERTISED on TV again today. For a small fortune, we can order a treasury of Christmas music sung by our favorite celebrities. Cheery, yes, but nothing can compare with live entertainment.

I refer to the peanut gallery's annual Christmas pageant. All over the planet, munchkins dressed in velvet and lace or spiffy three-piece suits stomp onto risers like a herd of baby elephants. Moments later, the room comes alive with ho-ho-hos. What the adorable choir lacks in talent, it makes up in enthusiasm. And volume.

With gusto, they race against the jaunty piano music and, more often than not, emerge victorious. Oblivious to the hundreds of eyes upon them, they scratch whatever itches or mine for a nasal nugget in between numbers. Oh, to be five years old with no use for propriety!

Some soloists shout their offerings into the microphone, while others are barely audible. And a little girl afflicted with stage fright forgets her lines altogether. The audience can count on an essential prop tumbling over or other major calamity. And halfway through the program, the mike causes one heck of a ruckus before fizzling out completely.

These are the trademarks of holiday programs in Anytown, USA. Yet they're one-of-a-kind moments to proud parents who chuckle at the unrehearsed mishaps, grateful for comic relief. It's more acceptable wiping away tears of laughter than those that mist from watching a child grow up.

I made all the usual newcomer mistakes at my son's first Christmas concert. Not having the foresight to ask where his class would be, I found myself seated on the opposite end of the room. Dirty looks trailed me as I excuse-me'd past a row of laps in order to take pictures. As a result, my rump starred in numerous home videos.

Unfortunately, my photos fell short of bringing the moment to life. Luckily, a friend gave me a copy of his production (Thanks, Bob!), which captured the program in all its charm. The elves, the music and the magic will live on forever in a standard videocassette.

I could order that treasury of Christmas tunes I saw on TV. After all, I turned the house inside out hunting for a pen to jot down the number.

But I think maybe I'll tear up that note and watch an old video instead.

OH, CHRISTMAS TREE!

TRADITION AND THE almighty dollar play important roles in the Great Christmas Tree Debate. Some people feel strongly that only a real *tannenbaum* symbolizes the season, while others are content with a fake metal one.

As a reporter of sorts, I researched both sides of the issue so that you, the consumer, could make an educated choice. Set forth below are my insightful findings.

Benefits Of Artificial Trees

1. You can put them up earlier—like, for instance, Arbor Day. Heck, you can leave 'em up all year if you want!

2. Their needles don't leave a telltale trail, thus inflicting puncture wounds in unsuspecting feet.

3. You can bend their branches in virtually any direction, which in itself is entertaining.

4. The biggest perk, however, is monetary relief. After paying a frightening one-time fee, you're set for life.

Benefits Of The Real McCoy

1. It smells nice.

2. You can't see a goofy metal pole running up the middle.

3. No well-meaning clod says, "It looks just like *real*!"

4. Three words: no assembly required.

For many people, tradition motivates them to buy one of the thirty-three million genuine, bona fide trees sold each year. They choose from two methods, depending on their ambition and tendency to procrastinate.

1. By visiting a local tree lot and selecting from a wide range of shapes and sizes; or

2. By chopping one down at a tree farm. This *Little House on the Prairie* approach appeals to a growing number of folks who've come to appreciate life's simple pleasures. Then they haul it home and set it up somewhere between the big-screen TV and their sprawling computer system.

But if they *really* want to get back to nature, they should grow their own from seed. Granted, it could take up to fifteen years, but think of the anticipation! Better yet, they could harvest it early and use it as a tabletop model.

Regardless of how it's acquired, experts advise keeping your tree away from heat sources. This includes fireplaces, radiators and ladies going through their change. They further recommend frequent watering. Depending on size, some trees absorb a gallon a day. For jumbo specimens, one may find an irrigation system in order.

Not one to challenge the experts, I made sure I gave our tree a generous drink every day last Christmas season. And now the darn thing's rusted.

THE PERFECT GIFT?

LAST MINUTE CHRISTMAS shoppers are under the gun now and area stores hope to cash in on the frenzy. Even the local head shop claims to offer something for everyone on your list.

Chances are, you'll settle for *anything* right now just to be done with it. You hear a festive ad on the radio and soon you're wrapping a jug of windshield washer fluid for that special someone. But...what if you're looking for the Perfect Gift—the one that will bring a twinkle to the eyes of your recipient?

The way I see it, he or she is partially responsible. Forget that surprise-me line. Anyone expecting a gift should be required by law to make a wish list in advance. This can be either oral or written, and length is optional. My husband's list consists of only one item—a gift certificate to the local hardware store. Consequently, he never has to shake his present much to guess its contents.

The trouble with giving gift certificates is there's no chance to fudge. Says right on there big as life that you paid fifty bucks for it. I Christmas shop all year long so I can find the perfect gift at a more reasonable price. Then I peel off a mound of clearance stickers so no one's the wiser (except those few who read my column).

Modern wish lists may take on an electronic form. I noticed Penney's and other companies offer an online registry now. People can log onto the site to zero in on their beloved's desire.

And while researching this column, I ran across another helpful site called Presentpicker.com. You plug in the personality of your intended receiver from dozens listed—for example: egotist, busybody, controlling, etc. Then you choose his or her interests from another box and, with a click of the rat, up pops an assortment of gift ideas.

But what about Santas who shun computers? My Better Half prefers the direct approach. "What do you want for Christmas?" he asked me the other day.

"A bath pillow and matching champagne glass," I replied.

"No, I mean seriously."

"I seriously want a bath pillow and matching champagne glass."

In the end, he convinced me I was wrong. So I logged on to Presentpicker.com to find out what I *really* want. And I'll gladly forward the list to anyone who's interested.

CURING THE AFTER-CHRISTMAS BLUES

IF YOU'RE ANYTHING like me, you routinely get the blues this time of year. After a steady injection of holiday hoopla, it's only natural to suffer from withdrawal.

I notice the first symptom moments after our last festive visit. Suddenly the tree, which once was the room's focal point, seems kind of in the way. And the gaily-wrapped gifts underneath morphed into a sprawling jumble of stuff I have no room for.

The day after Christmas finds me searching in vain for a parking spot. Then I push my way through a massive mob to stand in line at the customer service desk. I'm blown away by a blue light special announcing seventy-five percent off something I paid full price for two days prior. Then I return home to find the batteries died on the outrageously priced toy we gave our son. But that's okay because it broke anyway.

Inconspicuously, I unsnap my jeans, which fit tighter than normal from one too many parties. I eye up the glut of treats still hanging around, and ponder how to eat it all before my New Year's diet starts.

January 1st marks another tradition as well: tearing down the *tannenbaum*. Whereas adorning it marked a joyous occasion, I'm not too fond of the flip side. With a trembling lower lip, I carefully wrap the ornaments and tuck them in storage bags. Then I trudge up to the attic to deposit my sad sacks.

But wait! What's wrong with this picture? The first day of the year is no time to be glum! What we after-Christmas-blues sufferers need is something to look forward to. Like the old ketchup commercial, nothing perks us up like anticipation.

What better time than now to plan that summer vacation? The route, activities, you-name-it. Never mind it won't go as planned—do it anyway!

Or chart a map of this year's garden. The tomatoes go here...the cukes over there...and the weeds? Hmmm...how 'bout a smaller plot this year?

Or organize those holiday photos you took, as well as the millions languishing in a drawer somewhere.

What's that? Too tired? Then sit back with that novel you've been meaning to read. Better yet, write one yourself.

Whatever you do, take heart—it won't be long before those Christmas catalogs start arriving again. Two months, tops.

CHAPTER FOUR - IMAGINARY ENDING

THE BEARD LADY

I'M A BEARD LADY—not to be confused with "bearded," although I fret over that prospect now and then. What I mean is, I like men with beards. What attracted me most to my Better Half was his fine, furry face.

Guys grow beards for a variety of reasons. Perhaps the top motivator is an aversion to shaving. The excitement of that first shearing wears off all too soon. Young men also grow beards to look older. Older men may do it to look more distinguished. And a fair number of fellows develop facial hair just to feel macho.

So it struck me as odd when I learned that some guys dye their beards with women's hair color. Does he or doesn't he? That depends on the shade of the original growth. If it's not the hue he hoped for, he can opt for Midnight Black or Autumn Auburn. But only Mr. Clairol knows for sure.

Whatever the tint, beards should be well groomed. Like the 'do on top, they require regular shampooing. This prevents them from storing vittles for lengthy periods of time and smelling like my fridge did the time the power went out.

Like makeup, facial hair hides all sorts of imperfections. Is that complexion as smooth as gravel? Grow a full beard! And a mustache and goatee mask that oily T-area. Beards help camouflage a fleshy face, too. I know a guy who shaved off his distinguished-looking beard only to expose an *un*distinguished-looking set of chins. Quips from his colleagues convinced him to can the new look quickly.

One must exercise patience to grow a beard. And restraint. It's tempting to give up when the stubble itches like a massive mosquito bite. But guys are advised not to shave so much as a whisker for at least four weeks. After that point, the manly mane may be shaped as desired, with an eye toward recovering one's missing neck.

And to keep from looking like they just bagged a mastodon, frequent trims are recommended. These can be performed by a competent professional or a scissor-happy amateur, depending on the appearance they're striving for.

My husband, Dan, prunes his own beard. A snip-snip here and a snip-snip there. Twenty minutes later, he looks human again.

And because I like facial hair so much, I get to clean the sink.

THE BRAT CAT

I THOUGHT *I* WAS moody until Marble the Cat moved in. Like other felines, she practices her sweet little kitty routine, rubbing up against the nearest appendage. But when we reach down to stroke her royal head, she rewards us with a finger chomp. This effectively discourages heavy petting.

Marble made it transparent from day one that this was her domain, and she's reigned for well over a year now. One false move on our part and she puts us in our place with a resounding hiss.

Her favorite game is Ambush. Concealing herself on a dining room chair, she takes a swipe at anyone who happens by. She further entertains herself by swatting at us as we descend the stairs. Once she got a little carried away and tumbled off the railing. After a surprise landing, she gave it a dirty look and strutted away.

She'd have more time for trouble if not for her frequent naps. Cats need their beauty rest, of course. And after a siesta, she begins her exercise program. First she executes a few stretches, thereby doubling her body length. Then it's time for aerobics when her ears shift back and, with a wild look in her eyes, she hightails it up the stairs. Other times she races from room to room in the same reckless fashion only to slam into a wall. She recovers in short order and displays not the least bit of embarrassment.

Marble bravely harasses our feet when we stride across the floor. But if we suddenly turn around, the little coward slams on her brakes and makes a mad dash in the opposite direction. "You'd *better* run!" we holler, just to egg her on.

But nothing makes her accelerate like bedtime. When she senses I'm about to shut her in for the night, she darts behind the couch or under a bed. Then I extract my brat cat and cradle her in my arms, relishing my only triumph over her.

Living with a moody cat isn't easy, but there's one perk I enjoy. I read her facial expression, which never changes much, and verbalize her feisty thoughts. My role as interpreter allows me to be conceited ("Aren't I beau-*tee*-ful?") or theatrical ("I vant to be alone"). And when I'm demanding ("Hey! Where's the Chef's Blend?"), she generally gets her way.

Because when Marble talks, people listen.

CRIME AND FOOLISHNESS

IF THERE'S ONE line of work I'd be leery of, it's that of a career criminal. It may beat a nine-to-five job for excitement, but too many things can go wrong.

Take robbers, for instance. A twenty-four-year-old thief drove a truck away during a shift change at Saginaw County Mosquito Abatement Commission. But the pickup had a tracking device so authorities had no problem finding him. Now, what are the odds a bug truck would be bugged?

A crook in Salt Lake City sabotaged himself while robbing First Utah Bank. He pulled a gun from an envelope that also contained his diploma from an anger management course. Then he made off with nearly $35,000 but left the incriminating certificate behind. It's safe to assume he's *really* P-O'ed now.

No doubt, when fugitives flee, the adrenaline flows, but not necessarily to their brains. When Troy police chased a trio of bandits, the robbers threw rolls of coins at them. Eventually, they were apprehended and taken to head-*quarters*.

And the outfits these people wear! Hefty bags have apparently replaced ski masks on the felon fashion scene. A seventy-year-old woman slipped on a basic black garbage bag with eye- and armholes before trying to rob the Bank of Colorado. The garment nearly covered the four-foot eleven-inch bandit, who looked a trifle suspicious. Someone alerted police who promptly arrested her.

But thieves aren't the only trendsetters. When Allegan County police cornered a murder suspect, he was disguised in a sassy skirt and wig. All dressed up and no place to go.

Still others use weird weapons. A Clare, Michigan woman assaulted her boyfriend with a can of pork and beans. An unusual choice of weapon perhaps. But I've been victimized by Van Camps myself and it's no laughing matter.

Speaking of bodily discomfort, an Oregon drug dealer experienced his share when the cops stopped the car he rode in. While police questioned the occupants, the narcotics he'd hidden down his pants began burning his bottom. After squirming a while, he finally surrendered the drug. I'm gonna take a guess here and say it was crack.

But the strangest article I've read tells of a Mount Clemens man convicted of molesting three girls. Did I mention his age? A hundred and one. Which leads me to another reason for not being a career criminal

They never retire.

A FAIR WEATHER FIEND

I ONCE REGARDED it as an old-folks' activity, but lately my Better Half and I kick off our mornings by watching The Weather Channel. Dan prefers the local forecast, while my inquiring mind wants to know who'll get drenched or dumped on, as long as it's not me.

Despite being wrong half the time, the pair who share airtime ooze confidence as they tell us what atmospheric conditions to expect. Just once I'd like to hear them say, "Man, we really blew yesterday's forecast, didn't we? Son of a gun!"

They derive a considerable amount of dialogue from an unlikely looking weather map. "Here you see a warm air mass pushing its way through the west, which will produce yada-yada-yada..." And they keep on yakking, oblivious to that venomous-looking jet stream slithering behind them.

Inclement weather attracts viewers, so Dan says they play up those storm predictions to increase the ratings. We watched as one guy forecasted a blizzard that promised to close schools, businesses and possibly even the mall. And there wasn't a cloud in the sky! Now that takes guts. Just for the record, the storm never materialized. I bet Chicken Little had a tough time living that one down.

To be honest, I prefer the man-on-the street reporter whose beard frosts up as he describes the cold front that just moved in—as though it needs a description. Equally amusing is Horizontal Harry, who clings to a telephone poll while reporting a hurricane in progress. "It's a little windy out here, folks," he says, before a wind gust rips his microphone away.

Speaking of which, I have in my possession a six-year list of hurricane names—one hundred twenty-six handles in all—and I'm a little disgruntled my name's not on it. The World Meteorological Organization at its international meetings decides which names to use, so I'm submitting mine to the group and hope I don't get a rejection letter.

I get a little annoyed over conflicting weather reports, too. How can radio, newspapers and TV spew out vastly different predictions? Don't they use the same crystal ball? Day planners can either choose what's behind door number two or the ever popular eenie-meenie-miney-moe method. Personally, I pick the most favorable forecast and schedule my activities accordingly.

I guess that makes me a fair weather fiend.

GEE WHIZ! IT'S OPRAH!

IS THERE A CURE for Oprah-itis? I've been suffering from that malady for a while now.

Don't get me wrong—I greatly admire the lady's spunk and sense of humor. I'm inspired by her rags-to-riches story and humanitarian efforts. And her talk show beats the others, tongues down. But if I see her name on one more thing, I'm gonna Ope-chuck.

Of course, no one has to twist my arm to watch her late afternoon program. From feel-good episodes to celebrity interviews, I never fail to come away entertained and even a wee bit wiser. Like, so *what* if supper burns?

The show is created by Harpo Productions, Inc, of which Oprah is chairman. She also has her hands in Harpo, Inc., Harpo Films, Inc., Harpo Video, Inc. and Harpo Studios, Inc. It took me a mere decade to realize they're all Oprah spelled backwards.

In 1996, she launched her famous on-the-air book club to inspire people to read more. Every book she spotlighted became a bestseller, bringing instant fame to dozens of lucky authors. The Literary Guild reaped big dividends by labeling select books an Oprah pick. Why...my local library *still* devotes an entire bookcase to it.

As the credits from her show roll up, viewers are reminded they can buy transcripts of their favorite shows for five bucks. But there's a cheaper way to glean those highlights. Yes sirree, Bob, for folks who just can't get enough, Oprah has a web site now (www.oprah.com). Fans can access the site before the program starts to learn future themes. And they can log on after it airs to rehash the details and duke it out on a message board.

But wait! There's more! Oprah's most recent addition is...drum roll please... Oprah Magazine! It's simply called "O" as in "O, my gosh, this thing ain't cheap." The pricey periodical should be subtitled "All Ads All the Time." While it does contain some well-written articles, they're buried deeply beneath volumes of advertising. And I can't afford the products 'cause I blew my wad on her magazine.

Oprah's distinct handle has become such a household word, it surprised me to learn her *real* name is Gail. Gee whiz. Whodathunk?

GETTING AWAY FROM IT ALL

A TEAM LED BY Professor of Astronomy Geoffrey Marcy recently discovered some planets outside our solar system. They haven't yet been given real names such as Uranus. Just for the record, Webster's preferred pronunciation of that strange word accents the front syllable (as in YER-in-us) rather than the more popular rear end. No matter how you pronounce it, Uranus is often the butt of jokes. (Get it?)

But I digress. For identification purposes, one of the new planets has been dubbed UpsAndb. Goofy name aside, astronomers say the exciting revelation suggests that there could indeed be life beyond our galaxy.

You might ask, How does this affect me personally? And I would reply, "Summer travel season." Maybe you've noticed that our resorts burst with people of every size, shape and financial state. Airports swarm with folks on their way to heaven knows where. And highway traffic resembles the ants that spotted a crumb on my counter the other day.

Yes, one could journey a thousand miles to a remote cave only to meet a dozen tourists emerging. So much for getting away from it all.

Clearly, travelers need a new place to go—which is why the planet discovery is so appealing. Just imagine! When your boring friends brag about their pending cruise to Jamaica, you could one-up them with, "That's nothing—we're trekking to UpsAndb this year!"

But I'm getting ahead of myself. Before any tours could be launched, we'd need to iron out a few galactic wrinkles first. These include, but are not limited to: What kind of planet life are those astronomers referring to anyway? Are the natives friendly or do they make like Darth Vader? What (besides craters) are the tourist attractions? What is the exchange rate for U.S. currency? And of special interest to incontinent travelers and those with kids, how many restrooms can we expect on the hundred-bazillion-mile route?

Once the Powers-that-Be address these concerns, it won't be long before we can vacation out there in the final frontier. Chances are, spacebound families will still experience some travel frustrations. Husbands won't ask for directions and wives will gripe, "You were supposed to turn *left* at that asteroid!"

But the perks should outweigh the pains when we get away from it all in UpsAndb. And the view should be out of this world.

HEY MISTER, YA GOT TWO BITS?

MONEY CAN'T BUY love but it *can* buy...money?? Yes, folks, for a mere thirteen-ninety-five, you can own a highly polished set of five state quarters. Better yet, receive this collection absolutely free (value, a buck-twenty-five) with your purchase of a twenty-dollar collector's map (value, zip). What a deal!

For those who may have been locked in an attic, the United States Mint launched a decade-long tribute to this great country of ours. Each year it's honoring five states with commemorative quarters. To be fair (and avoid a potential civil war), these will be unveiled in the order that their respective states joined the union. In other words, don't hold your breath hunting for Hawaii.

Only a limited number of these quarters will be minted, so they're sure to become valuable. Experts estimate their future worth to be in the neighborhood of twenty-five cents (not counting inflation).

Like many of the country's gullible citizens, I've climbed on the state-quarter bandwagon. But unlike some people, I prefer the thrill of the hunt. In January, I hooted with glee when I found the final quarter in last year's set. I'd rather discover them myself than buy a package of gleaming specimens. That's like an angler shopping at a fish market. My coins may be a little scuffed, but that just adds to their charm.

I admit I considered buying the aforementioned seventeen-inch by twenty-eight inch, extra thick, double ply collector's map with brushed aluminum edges. But where do you stick something like that? Another option I stumbled over was a handsome, twenty-five dollar leather book that holds your twelve dollars and fifty cents' worth of coins. But for some reason I balked at that, too. Until I find a display that doesn't cost more than its contents, I'm hoarding my treasures in an exquisite plastic coin purse with a rigid clasp and authentic tattered lining.

Every so often I take them out and admire them. We numismatics like to do that. Ol' George still graces the head of each quarter, but the eagle won't land on the "tails" side any time soon.

Instead, each state will furnish a unique design that will appear on roughly a bazillion quarters. And before you know it, they'll make their way to my dinky hometown.

Then with tin cup poised, I'll stand on a corner and holler, "Hey, mister! Ya got two bits?"

THE HOLIDAY FROM HADES

HAND IN HAND, a sun-bronzed couple sprints along the shore of what looks like Paradise. (This occurs in slow motion, of course—no one hurries when they're on vacation, right?) And somehow, this thirty-second commercial spurs a few thousand people to visit their nearest travel agent.

Unlike us Corcorans, most folks seem to live for their next adventure. They head north, south, east and west—to the mountains, the seas and every tourist trap in between. But after spending shameless amounts of moolah, they return to describe the Holiday from Hades.

A friend of mine, and her extended family, just came back from a cruise. They counted the days 'til their exciting excursion but, once aboard, tempers flared due to the close confinement. One person refused to do this activity and another rejected something else. The bickering escalated until their countdown resumed—this one marking the *end* of their luxury trip.

Those getting-back-to-nature vacations can be just as taxing. Unless you do it every day, erecting a tent demands a substantial number of brain cells. The seasoned camper plans ahead for an invasion of mosquitoes. Furthermore, you can expect a ninety-eight percent chance of a monsoon, during which you recall your tepee leaks.

Whatever your destination, chances are Murphy's Law will mess things up good. And it matters not what mode of transportation you choose.

Frugal travelers favor driving, but that presents its own set of problems. You can count on the A/C to conk out five minutes into the trip. And a broken fan belt means sightseeing at some picturesque service station. Add to that, construction zones and backseat fighting and you have a classic case of road trip rage.

Air travel is considerably faster, but can result in lost luggage, delayed flights and pilots dozing off. Hey, it's true! In a report issued by Allied Pilots Association, a sleep-deprived pilot admitted he 'faded fast' somewhere over Mexico. Where's a snooze alarm when you need one?

Given the calamities that sabotage a normal vacation, you'd think people would choose to stay home. But instead, *National Geographic Adventure* magazine recently presented the twenty-five greatest adventures in the world. These include such pleasures as rigorous cosmonaut training in Russia, and hundred-mile-a-day hikes through Tanzania.

I can't wait to see the commercial.

THE LITTLE ENGINE THAT COULDN'T

THE MOST EFFECTIVE lessons in life are those learned the hard way. This is especially true when it comes to automobiles.

A friend reported that her teenage daughter now understands the wisdom of owning a spare set of keys. This knowledge grew from locking herself out of her car during the bowels of winter—with the engine running.

A coupon for french fries prompted another pal to visit her local Burger King. Her good fortune ended, however, when she pulled up too close to the take-out window and clipped the curb. The resulting blown tire spurred her husband to replace all four, bringing the total cost of her free meal to two hundred and fifty dollars.

Car trouble happens to all of us. But for reasons I can't fathom, significant others of the male persuasion like to accuse us ladies of screwing up—as though *they* never make automotive mistakes. And just how do they explain that mounting gas cap collection at the self-serve station?

Our blameless guys' first reaction, more often than not, is "What did you *do*?" This results in rampant paranoia. And while I may snap, "I didn't *do* anything," deep down I'm thinking, *Geez—I wonder what I did this time...*

Last week, I turned the key in Old Faithful's ignition, only to hear deafening silence. Accordingly, I suspected operator error. *Maybe I didn't rotate it far enough,* I thought, but half a dozen attempts convinced me otherwise. *Oh, no!* my mind raced. *I must've left the headlights on!* But I hadn't. Satisfied that the battery had simply exhausted its long, boring life, I dismissed the matter.

I have to give credit to my Better Half. Despite his suspicions, he kept silent for a change. But when Dan the Man replaced our Diehard, the dome light promptly lit up.

Car maintenance is another one of those hard-won lessons, although it appears many of us haven't caught on yet. According to the Vehicle Maintenance Council, four out of five cars on the road need service. This can mean anything from a simple oil change to replacing the transmission. The council further recommends using our senses to detect car trouble. If you *hear* a curious rattle, *smell* oil burning, *feel* your vehicle shake or *see* the engine on fire, it's time to take ol' Bessie in.

Unless, of course, you're sense-*less*.

LOOKING FOR LOOKERS?

I SCAN THE PERSONAL ads on occasion, not because I'm looking. but because I find them entertaining. While most are placed by nice, sincere singles looking for other nice, sincere singles, a few of them give me pause to say, "Huh?"

I'm all for honesty, but had to chuckle at the lady who counted shopping among her interests. She sought a financially secure guy—no doubt so she could further that hobby.

An ad run by 'Starting Over' who said he was recovering from a broken heart, set off red flags, too. He may as well say, "Let's go out so I can talk about my ex."

Then there's the red-blooded American woman seeking "an attractive, dark haired, well-built guy." Her ad's caption should have read, 'Looking for Lookers.'

Some ads specifically no chemical dependency. Obviously, asthmatics don't want to don an oxygen mask for a candlelight dinner. And smokers don't have to carry a torch to be detected—their telltale aroma gives them away. But what about drug users? Who in their right mind would admit to that? Unless, of course, their date requires a whiz test.

A few ads allow social drinking, which I assume means one doesn't sit home alone and get looped. Others forbid it in any form. I took offense to a divorced male's ad for a tall, non-drinker, who "despises the Internet." Wanted to call and say, "Hey, Bub, good things come in small packages! And another thing—I happen to *like* the World Wide Web, so don't knock it! Now if you'll excuse me, it's Miller Time."

A fair share of women list movies, dancing and dining out as their favorite pastimes. It seems to me they should forget about guys and just go out in a group. And give me a call while they're at it.

Guys, on the other hand, have a whole 'nother set of hobbies. One man said he enjoys fast cars, baseball, football, hockey, basketball, fishing and hunting. Did I mention he likes sports? And does he *really* think he's gonna find a girl who shares all of those interests?

Just for the heck of it, I wrote my own ad.

"Forty-something female, five-foot-two, blue eyes, hair color varies. Likes to eat, drink and be merry. Looking for someone to foot the bill."

I wonder if I'd get any takers?

LOW KARATE

SINCE THE TERRORIST attack, people have taken a renewed interest in martial arts—not to be confused with Marshall Dillon, who's a whole 'nother 'smoke. (Get it? *Gun*smoke.) Class sizes have swelled with folks eager to learn how to kick butt.

Not wanting to get left behind, I consulted a book I've owned for decades but never read called *Self Defense for Girls and Women* (Bruce Tegner and Alice McGrath, authors). In most of the photos, a big lug remains motionless while a ninety-eight pound lass engages in mortal combat.

I'm guessing that a real attacker might be more mobile and may scoff at requests to stand still. To prepare for that outside possibility, the guide stresses the need for practice. 'Be careful not to hurt your partner,' it warns frequently, so those winding up in traction won't sue the publisher for medical expenses.

As a public service, I present here some key maneuvers I learned. At the risk of discriminating, I'll refer to the aggressor as "he" for purposes of consistency and because males are generally more aggressive than females. So...what should you do to the naughty man?

Stay out of grabbing range by side-kicking his shin or knee with the arch of your foot. Forget those high, dramatic kicks on TV—this is more of a "low karate" move.

If the hoodlum is behind you, jab him with an elbow blow to the abdomen. If no "Oomph!" results, feel free to supply the necessary sound effects.

For a good face-to-face tactic, connect the fingers and thumb of your favorite hand and slightly cup your palm. Then apply a karate chop to the crook of his arm, the side of his neck or under his nose. Better yet, all three.

And here's another hand-y move: Finger stab him in the eyes. For pointers, watch *The Three Stooges*.

The handy little paperback describes a few variations of these techniques as well as one called the Finger Pull. At first I balked at this trick, having fallen for it numerous times, but it's a far cry from my Better Half's antics. To execute it, you must grab the punk's pinky and yank it back and forth. Unless he's made of bionic parts, this will hurt like heck.

With a little luck, surprising your attacker with these strategies will help you subdue him. At least so you can run to the safety of Marshall Dillon.

A PLOY NAMED SUE

THERE ARE MORE drug ads on TV these days than, well, Carter has pills. But have you noticed they're not like normal commercials? The first half encourages us to buy the product, but the *last* half talks us *out* of it. ("Some people may experience pimples, malaria, halitosis, death and other symptoms...") Seems to me that kind of defeats the purpose.

This CYA-type marketing hopes to thwart our love affair with litigation. Otherwise some unsuspecting consumer could say, "You guys never *told* me I'd get hemorrhoids from this!" and—bingo!—another frivolous lawsuit. Or, as I like to call 'em, flawsuits.

As a former legal secretary, I've seen some interesting cases, but nothing like the ones I've heard about lately. One involves a Livonia woman who sued her *deceased* ex-husband for stalking. She claimed that, though he doesn't get around much any more, she's still afraid of him. I assume she wanted the million-dollar settlement to hire a dead bodyguard.

In the holier-than-thou department, an inmate sued the Michigan Department of Corrections for wrongful incarceration on the grounds that he's God. How, he reasoned, could he be guilty of robbery if he owns the entire planet? Hhmm...good point...

Another inmate sued a prison claiming its food caused him excessive flatulence, thus bringing new meaning to the term 'gas chamber.'

In fact, vittles are often the subject of controversy. A practicing Hindu sued Taco Bell when the restaurant accidentally served him a beef burrito. He alleged this caused emotional distress, medical expenses and loss of wages. I'm a vegetarian myself, but I know bull when I hear it.

It's almost as though people are *waiting* for something to happen so they can cash in on a legal jackpot. And if nothing comes their way, they take matters into their own hands—or other body parts, as the case may be. Take the student who sued an Idaho college for failing to warn him of the dangers of third-floor dorms. Otherwise, he never would have tried mooning his pals out the window.

Perhaps most bizarre of all is the Michigan man who claimed that a car accident rendered him gay. And I *don't* mean happy. Although chances are he was pretty joyful over his two hundred thousand dollar settlement.

To these plaintiffs and others itching to sue, I say, go take a pill. Just remember: May cause drowsiness...

A WILDER BLUE YONDER

WHEN I FIRST HEARD the term sky rage, an ominous scene crossed my mind. I pictured P-O'ed pilots duking it out in the wild, blue yonder and firing pistols at the sorry cuss who cut them off.

I was relieved to learn it's disgruntled *passengers* responsible for this somewhat recent trend. Why are they disgruntled? Often, it's a case of too much alcohol. Combine that with a ban on smoking, smaller airline seats, long ticket counter lines and flight delays, and you have a Mad Max on your hands. Just wait 'til he finds out his luggage is lost.

Regardless of the reason, these cranky customers are wreaking serious havoc in the sky. Take for example Gerard Finnerman, a Connecticut businessman traveling first class. His demand for more alcohol was denied, so he shoved a flight attendant aside and served himself. Then he used the service cart for a commode and finished the job with a fine linen napkin. I'd hate to see what he'd do in coach.

In another incident, a passenger walked up and down the aisle screaming, "We're all gonna die! This plane is gonna crash!" Then the optimist threw a flight attendant over three rows of seats. This needlessly upset other travelers and didn't do much for the stewardess either.

Even Reverend Robert Schuller raised some Cain. While fighting over where to hang his robe, he smacked a flight attendant and subsequently paid a fine. He's lucky he didn't wind up in the pokey. Sky rage antics are punishable by up to twenty years in prison, where the service is even worse.

Not only can perpetrators land in jail, they jeopardize their lives and the lives of other passengers. When pilots of small crafts leave the cockpit to restrain a troublemaker, ain't no one flyin' that plane.

Chances are, these people don't *plan* to make a spectacle of themselves. They just get carried away by circumstances. With summer travel season upon us, here are some tips for keeping a lid on air travel stress:

1. Forget the alcohol. People at thirty thousand feet don't need to get any higher.

2. If you smoke, chew nicotine gum for a puffless fix.

3. Put that laptop away and focus on something more relaxing. Like the air sickness bag.

4. Stand up and stretch. Better yet, take a stroll up the aisle. But don't bother the pilot. He's busy tailgating a Cessna.

WRITING AN IMAGINARY ENDING

A SHOW I WATCHED last evening kept me awake all night. True, I should have known better. Movies based on a true violent incident usually *contain* a true violent incident. And, like most of today's films, this one realistically portrayed the event. Thus, I realistically portrayed an insomniac.

Frankly, I liked it better when movies left the details to our imagination. In the original version of *Psycho*, did we actually view Janet Leigh being carved up? Heck, no. We saw a silhouette behind a shower curtain. And the fake blood trickling down the drain was of the less shocking black-and-white variety.

The same goes for mating. We all knew what Rhett had in mind when he carried Scarlet up the staircase. No steamy boudoir scene would get the point across any clearer. Today's soap operas could take a lesson from ol' Rhett—and focus on the plot instead of the cot.

Likewise in the movie *Oh God*, the visual does no justice to the mental image. John Denver was deeply disappointed when the Lord showed up looking like George Burns.

Using our imaginations can enhance life, but the older we get, the less we are called on to do so. Even children's fantasies are in jeopardy these days, and movies aren't the only culprits. When I was a kid, dolls were lucky if they could drink and wet, and I had to invent anything beyond that realm. Now they do everything but smoke (and sue the tobacco industry).

When my family built a snowman last winter, I used my imagination to round up body parts that would bring him to life. (For those with their minds in a gutter, I mean *above* the waistline.) Instead of sporting ordinary peepers, our frigid fellow looked comical in a pair of ski goggles. As someone easily amused, I chuckled every time I looked at him.

So you can imagine my surprise when I found a snowman kit in a catalog. For fifteen bucks, customers receive the manufactured version of Frosty's facial features. But why should we make our sculptures conform to someone's idea of perfection? Sounds like a horror flick—*The Stepford Snowmen*.

We must take action to preserve our collective imaginations. Accordingly, I'd like you all to put down your newspapers and do the following exercise: Now...try to think of an ending for this column.

Then *I* won't have to.

~ * ~

I Hate To Gripe, But...

Lois A. Corcoran

Hard Shell Word Factory

Trade paperback
Published January 2007

© 2006 Lois A. Corcoran
eBook ISBN-10: 0-7599-4787-2
eBook ISBN-13: 978-0-7599-4787-0
Published October 2006

Hard Shell Word Factory
PO Box 161
Amherst Jct. WI 54407
books@hardshell.com
www.hardshell.com
Cover art © 2006 Dirk A. Wolf

CHAPTER 1 – ONCE UPON A QUALITY TIME

DON'T SHOOT THE PIANO TEACHER

WE SAT THERE quietly on the couch, minding our own bee's wax, when suddenly there occurred an unearthly clamor. Investigation revealed that the piano bench, which held some five hundred pounds of sheet music, had finally caved in. Thus, an instrument that had lived in relative obscurity was promptly brought to our attention.

'Til now, our upright piano had spent fifteen years hidden in a dark nook in the dining room. Perhaps "hidden" isn't the proper word for a five-foot-square fixture. But we tended to overlook (if not downright ignore) it.

"Let's move it to the living room," said my Better Half, and I agreed. Since then it has become a focal point instead of a candidate for Lemon Pledge. One can't enter the parlor now without an overwhelming urge to tackle the ivories.

Even our son, Kelly, who won't touch a thing without a mouse attached, has been drawn to it and requested I give him lessons. Having never taken them myself, it's a bit like the blonde leading the blonde. But we have this cool book called *Usborne Piano Course* that is virtually goof proof.

With it, we're learning note names and proper fingerings one at a time. Not surprisingly, the first few songs sounded pretty much the same. But we've since graduated to classic toe tappers like "Mary Had a Little Lamb."

We're also becoming acquainted with a number of musical terms. The word piano, for instance, actually means "quiet" in Italian. Obviously the Italians never heard us play. We use only two volumes: forte and fortissimo (also known as loud and louder).

Furthermore, some of the lower notes are painfully out of tune. Our "Baby Elephant Walk" sounds like it tripped and fell. And ought to be in traction. On the plus side, this provides a valid excuse when a melody doesn't sound right.

We also "blame that tune" on acoustics and other assorted alibis. So *sue* me! Just don't shoot the piano teacher.

Maybe we're not quite ready for Carnegie Hall or the cover of the

Rolling Stone. But we *have* had a chance to play a duet. I hate to toot my own horn but our quarter notes didn't sound half bad. As a whole.

ONCE UPON A QUALITY TIME

MAYBE YOU'VE SEEN the commercial. A twenty-something babe lounges on a couch in front of a fire, absently stirring her tea. Her kids just braved the cold to board a school bus, so she faces a tranquil day ahead. And wrapped in this cozy setting, she has the gall to say, "Being a mom is a tough job."

Come again? Try moving out to the trenches, lady. I did that recently when I resolved to spend more quality time with the family this year. Our only son turned ten and I yearned for some old-fashioned, Walton-type togetherness. So we brainstormed and came up with a few weekly events sure to please John-Boy and Mary Ellen.

For Reading Night, I spread out afghans on the floor, adding pillows for cushy comfort, and there we camp with a stack of books. Before long we're each engrossed in our own selection.

But just when I get to a good part, Kelly yells, "Hey, Mom, listen to this...!" Then through spasms of laughter he reads a Dave Barry passage aloud. "Little heed would...(*Hee-Hee!*)...make a good name for a...(*Ha-Ha-Ha!*)...rock band (Snicker-*Guffaw!*)"

The first dozen times this happened I smiled obligingly, but soon the interruptions became annoying. "Okay, okay—time to read to yourself," I said, and things quieted down. So much so that I drifted off to sleep. And missed our quality time completely.

Movie Night is great in theory, too. It may consist of:
(a) a trip to the theater, complete with snacks and beverage. When the beverage wants "out," of course, there's no Pause button to facilitate the potty break. To make matters worse, Michael Jordan sits in front of us, blocking the view. And since the total value of the deal could fund a new car, we sometimes opt for...

(b) renting videos. This means agreeing on which of thousands to choose from. No one likes the wholesome, feel-good entertainment I pick out, and I'm not fond of *their* choices. Nevertheless, we strike a compromise and sit back to watch a mutually tolerable show. But when a funny scene occurs, the men of the house replay it over and over, effectively driving me insane.

Next time it happens, I'm gonna join that tranquil, tea-stirring

Mom. I guess she had the right idea after all.

PLAYING CHESS DAY AND KNIGHT

THANKS TO HARRY Potter, my ten-year-old son is charmed with chess these days. In the movie, the medieval pieces come to life to battle each other. Though we combed the stores, we've yet to find a set that animated.

I never realized how popular and high-tech the game has become. The ancient theme gets lost in today's beeping hand-held devices. Knights of Yore would turn over in their armor if they knew. Computer chess offers nifty special effects, but nothing beats a real live game.

I judge a chess set by its players. If there are well-formed little horsies, I consider it worth our wealth. At least to a point. I'd have to be a queen to afford some of them. We settled for your basic plastic set that's light enough to go anywhere. You can even set it up outdoors provided there's no wind.

Owning a chess set is one thing. Playing is quite another. No matter how often Kelly briefs me on the rules, they never sink in. I have a hard enough time remembering which piece is which, let alone where to stick it.

If I recall correctly, the rook can move by rank or file, which are fancy terms for sideways or up-and-down. Furthermore, numbers identify the ranks, while letters distinguish the files. "Rook to B-5," Kelly announced the other day.

"Bingo!" I yelled.

Though it's politically incorrect, I can see why they call it The Thinking Man's Game. I can't advance a pawn without an hour of concentration. After carefully weighing my options one day, I performed what I thought was a safe maneuver.

Seconds later, Kelly made his move. "I just forked you," he said.

"You watch your mouth!" I replied.

"No, Mom. That means I can capture one of your pieces no matter what your next move is." While he trains me in terminology, I'm teaching him the virtues of winning with grace and losing with dignity. So far I've had loads of experience with the latter. Consequently, he yearns for some *real* competition and ambushes everyone he meets. "Hey!" he says as though he just thought of it. "Wanna play chess??"

He could duel day and knight. And I suspect he'll enjoy it long after Harry Potter hits The Late Late Show.

As for me, I think I'll stick with checkers.

ROASTING CHESS NUTS

NICE GAME, CHESS. But as a means of excitement, it ranks right up there with folding laundry. So I felt reasonably safe in suggesting my son start his own club. "You could call it The Chess Nuts," said I.

I pictured a hushed setting with several games in progress, each player deep in thought over his next move. And the club certainly *began* quietly enough. This was due in part because no one came the first week. But word got around and, for the next meeting, one whole person showed up. Eventually, the two-man guild grew to include five lively lads.

Due to the uneven number, the last one to arrive can either beep his way through electronic chess or harass the other players. The first ten minutes or so pass in relative peace, but soon I hear signs of discord like, "Hey, that's not fair! You didn't say 'check!'"

"I did, too!"

"You did not!"

Then they turn to me to settle the spat, despite the fact I know naught about the game.

"Do I look like I'm wearing stripes?" I ask, and leave them to duke it out themselves. Hence I learned what a rowdy pastime chess can be.

I may need work in the referee department, but I shine as Wonder Waitress even without the luxury of tips. In that capacity, I keep their bottomless bowls of "chess chips" full and dispense chocolate milk to boys who drink it by the cow-ful.

After reducing the snack to a few displaced crumbs, someone announces he's bored. This is the group's cue to stampede over to the pinball machine in the rec room. (Accurate name, that. By the time they leave, it *is* a (w)rec(k).) Either that or they share great literature in the form of Garfield comics. In fact—and this surprised me a bit—the chess club plays very little chess.

As reliable as the Pony Express, even a blizzard doesn't keep The Chess Nuts from their appointed rounds. And whereas it took weeks for the guys to start coming, they now are in no hurry to leave. Groans and long faces greet moms who come to pick them up, though some of the ladies stick around to chat.

"So...who won the chess match?" someone inevitably asks. Chess match? *What* chess match?

THE WIZARD OF OUNCE?

MY TEN-YEAR-OLD SON issued a wise piece of advice last summer. "Never watch a fish being cleaned just before lunch."

Thus launched a year full of insightful comments, most of which stemmed from home school. As luck would have it, my only student turned out to be the class clown.

"I'm not sure why, but the abbreviation for ounce is o-z," I told him in math one day.

"Then it must be 'The Wizard of Ounce,'" Kelly quipped.

Story problems prompted loads of observations. "If Hansel ate seventy-two pieces of gingerbread," he read obligingly from his textbook. "Then he's gonna get fat," he finished.

Among other things, science brought a study of animals, one of which was the ibex. "That sounds more like a drug to me," my son said, before breaking into his best announcer voice. "Ask your doctor if Ibex is right for you."

We also learned more than we wanted to know about the organs that make up our guts. "In other words," Kelly reasoned, "if I don't like someone, I could say, 'I hate your digestive system.'"

"Hmmm...I suppose so."

After a unit on weather, I quizzed him with, "And when do air masses occur?"

Without missing a beat, he answered, "When someone farts in church."

"Kelly Patrick," I yelled. "Now cut that out!"

"Do you know who Ben Franklin is?" I asked him one day.

"Of course," he replied with a straight face. "He's a store."

Then there was the history report he wrote called "The Irritating Iroquois."

"Why were they irritating?" I asked.

"They killed lots of people."

"Yeah, that could be annoying," I agreed.

My husband, Dan, launched a lesson in personal hygiene with this intro. "Kell, you're at an age now when you want to look your best, right?"

"No," he replied.

Every so often Kelly breaks out with the joke *du jour*. One time he asked, "What part of the house should you hold a rummage sale in?"

"Beats me."

"The cellar—get it? *Sell*-er?"

At a recent event, another mom told me, "Your son articulates so well."

"Thanks," I said. "I just wish he wouldn't articulate so *much*."

THE B.M. CLUB

WHEN OPRAH DISSOLVED her book club, it displaced millions of faithful members. Forced to fend for themselves, they roamed aimlessly through the streets not knowing what to read. To resolve the situation, I wanted to reinstate the nation-wide guild and include, as a bonus, film watching. In essence, it would be a Book and Movie club. Or B.M. for short.

Every good book becomes a motion picture eventually. For that matter, so do a whole lot of crummy ones. So it follows that after our intimate group of, say, ten million finishes the novel of the month, we'd party it up at local theaters. We'd conduct ourselves as adults, of course. No racing down the aisles or throwing popcorn like I did last week. (C'mon! I picked it up, didn't I?)

Older fiction may mean renting a dusty video and packing as many viewers as possible onto our sunken couch. After the final credits and cat hair removal, we could launch the age-old debate over which was better, the "B" or the "M".

Before going public with the B.M. club idea, I thought it best to test it on a smaller scale. So as a party of one, I waded through Jules Verne's classic, *Journey to the Center of the Earth*. The cover showed three guys clinging to a raft for dear life, their faces reflecting understandable concern. Naturally, I expected an action-packed adventure, but to be honest, I found it—dare I say?—boring.

Apparently, Hollywood had the same impression because the video had naught in common with the book. Old Professor Hardwigg changed his name and morphed into a younger, more virile kind of guy. When a fetching woman asked to join the expedition, he reluctantly—yeah, right—agreed. This provided the love interest Jules carelessly omitted from his novel.

Mr. Verne also made no mention of scantily clad natives inhabiting the earth's core, some of whom conveniently spoke English. Even the ending changed. A volcano was supposed to belch them out—or at least I think so. The book's narrator blacked out toward the end, cleverly eliminating the need for details.

All things considered, it was the perfect choice for a first B.M.

ANOTHER CENTS-LESS ARTICLE

"DARN!" HE SAID convincingly. "I forgot my wallet." But the convenient memory loss occurred on a regular basis. Thus, my husband Dan's crony skated out of paying for most golf games.

"What a cheapskate," I said when I heard about the guy's tactics. "Imagine pulling that stunt on your own friends! By the way—could you float me a few bucks 'til payday?"

As bookkeeper by default, I manage the moolah around these parts. The bills get paid when I don't misplace them, and I balance the checkbook each month. At first I found it difficult, but now I can steady it on my nose for well over a minute.

We both *write* checks, however, so each of us knows when we're in the hole. The other day Dan pointed out how much easier it is to calculate when there's a negative balance. "Then we can add checks instead of subtracting them," he said. Using that logic, our register was a cinch to cipher this month.

On Fridays when I'm not dodging overdraft notices, I dish out the family dough. "Here's your allowance," I say to Dan, who finds the phrase demeaning. He's fairly free with it and often gives himself an advance. At press time, he was tapping into the year 2010.

As for me, I must have been a rodent in a previous life. I squirrel away my loot and am rather nutty about parting with it. Our son, Kelly, takes after me in that respect. He stockpiles his for months at a time and has enough to stuff a bunk bed.

Besides his allowance, he earns a penny for each math problem he answers right. Consequently, I've been pretty cents-less lately. The catch—he has to pay one back for every mistake. Still, at thirty cents a day, he could make fifty-four tax-free dollars by the end of the school year.

I wondered if we were giving him too much 'til I read an article on the issue. It said the average nine to eleven-year-old receives seven bucks a week. But Janet Bodnar, author of *Dollars & Sense for Kids*, suggests giving children a weekly allowance equal to half of their age.

Based on that method, I deserve a raise.

SKIP TO MY LOO

MOST PEOPLE CREDIT Thomas Crapper for its invention, but that's a myth. In truth, an employee of his, Albert Giblin, deserves the honor. Or, in this case, the blame. Our temperamental toilet has been a source of conflict since the day it moved in.

Moments after installing it, Dan ushered me to the water closet for a lecture on the proper way to flush.

"Trust me," I said. "I'm familiar with the process."

Ignoring my comment, he continued. "You've gotta push down *gently* on the handle 'til you hear it swallow."

A distasteful picture came to mind. "I'll thank you to use a different word."

One day I made it 'swallow' twice in a row, which prompted another debate.

"Why did you do that?" Dan asked.

"So no one would—ah—hear anything."

"Do you realize it costs us seven-and-a-half *cents* per flush?"

I know I'm in trouble when the subject turns to money.

"Gosh, no," I replied. "Next time I'll wait'll it goes on sale."

We solved the sound effects problem by installing a musical trophy fish. Since then, Big Mouth Billy Bass has muffled the audio when necessary. But he did nothing to solve a recent complication.

If we didn't apply just the right amount of pressure to the handle, the head ran *ad infinitum*. Since loo leaks can waste two hundred gallons of water a day, the development prompted Dan to issue a new decree: No flushing unless it's "absolutely necessary." I'll leave the specifics to your imagination.

After a few days, Dan broke down and fixed the fickle fixture. Even so, there's no way our commode will last us fifty years, which is the appliance's ideal lifespan, according to the National Association of Home Builders.

In order to keep your porcelain pal that long, the guild offers these pointers: Never stand on the lid. (I don't recommend reclining either.) Never brace yourself against the tank. (No comment.) And don't use it for an "anything goes" garbage disposal.

Consequently, I've always taken great pains not to purge anything remotely iffy. So you can imagine my horror when a rock I'd pocketed for my ten-year-old tumbled out and landed at the bottom of the bowl. *After* a performance. It was with great reluctance that I fished it out.

Had I not, I knew I'd be "head"-ed for trouble.

SLIGHT-SEEING ON VACATION

OUTSIDE OF FREQUENT trips to our summer shack, our family has never taken what you'd deem a vacation. So imagine my excitement when my groom agreed to a cruise. Well...sort of. Instead of a love boat to Mazatlan, we'd hop a ferry to Mackinac Island.

The night before leaving, I crammed our luggage with essentials for the two-day trip, and sunshine greeted us as we made our departure.

Clouds moved in and a few raindrops splattered our windshield. Before long, my son and I tired of scenery and turned to reading.

"Look at that log cabin!" Dan yelled in an effort to regain our attention. This was followed by a succession of breaking news bulletins like, "Look at that... (insert one: truck...field...manure)!"

"Look at 'em yourself," I said after one too many interruptions.

By the time we settled into our motel room, rain pelted down. Hurrying to the dock, we dodged puddles the size of Lake Michigan. As luck would have it, we missed the boat by thirty seconds. A soggy half hour later, we boarded a catamaran, in lieu of an ark, and sped to the island in fourteen minutes flat.

I forked out good money for a rain slicker, which in truth was a glorified trash bag with armholes. I also bought souvenir placemats because they were practical and—need I say?—waterproof.

We toured the island via a horse-drawn carriage. Its vertical rain flaps failed to prevent a cold mist from chilling us die-hard tourists. Furthermore, they steamed up as soon as we boarded. Hence we saw little on our slight-seeing tour, save for the massive behinds of Billie and Bob.

"I wish we would've needed the sunblock we packed," Kelly declared in between shivers.

"Me, too," I said, recalling the shorts I brought for nothing.

But our motel stay made up for our Mackinac miseries. As Kelly played pinball in the resident arcade, Dan called my attention to its security camera. Like good tourists, we smiled and waved to the viewing audience.

We also used the pool and helped ourselves to a breakfast smorgasbord the next morning. And the disposable drinking cups in our room have a new home now. The only matching set we own, I might add. So what if they have the Budget Host logo on 'em?

With hospitality like that, you can bet we'll return. The next time we go slight-seeing.

ABCS OF CATCHING ZS

FORTY MILLION AMERICANS and I suffer from insomnia. From a gander at sleep aids on the market, some of us go to great lengths to summon slumber.

A rather bizarre remedy involves filling a muslin bag with dried hops and placing it under your pillow. Just for the record, filling a mouth with WET hops is discouraged...

...which reminds me of another sleep aid. You may recall a true story I told some years back when the beer my hubby brewed, exploded. On that occasion, my new ear plugs passed muster and I heard not a single bottle shatter.

But ear plugs have a down side, too. Dan often chooses the moment after I insert them to launch a conversation.

"What?" I say, pointing to the plugs. "I can't hear you." Then I grudgingly pull them out only to find he was lip syncing.

An eye mask does for eyes what ear plugs do for ears. True, you look like a raccoon in it, but it keeps out the glare of overzealous night lights. And it sure beats the sunglasses I've been wearing.

To catch some Zs, a book on natural healing recommends what I call The Three Ys: yoga, yogurt and ylang-ylang. (Okay—technically, that's *four* Y's.) What is ylang-ylang? Strangely enough, I anticipated that question. Ylang-ylang is an essential oil, meaning you *must* have it. When added to bathwater, it helps induce sleep—hopefully *after* you've crawled out of the tub.

And speaking of H_2O, a temperature-controlled waterbed can entice the sandman, too. It feels like you're drifting on an air mattress—with no fear of an offshore wind. I'd buy one myself if our hose reached upstairs.

And for those who will pay any price for comfort, there's a bed you can adjust to any position. The TV ad shows a couple sitting upright, enjoying a variety of activities. But that contradicts what I've heard about using beds only for slumber. People who routinely play cards in bed should ask their bridge club to meet elsewhere.

Then there's the sleep aid that is virtually free. Counting is an old remedy for insomnia, but it's not necessary to tally sheep. You could count the money in your mattress, for instance. Or count Dracula. Just don't count the calories you ate.

Or you could be up all night.

HASTEN TO THE BASIN

THEY SAY THAT fish and visitors stink after three days, but I could add one more to that list. Don't breathe near folks who redo their bathtubs either.

It all started when I got fed up with our old, porous basin. Nothing short of steel wool would clean the darn thing. Finally, one day I announced my plans to re-finish it.

"Yeah, right," said Dan. "That's an old trick women use to get their husbands to do something."

"Is that so?" I replied. "Well it just so happens I *am* going to do this myself."

He laughed a male-chauvinist laugh and escorted me to Menards for supplies. I assumed the shopping trip would go quickly. As it turned out, we spent several hours in the sandpaper department alone.

"Tell me again," I said when we arrived home, "why we need sandpaper to paint a tub."

He explained the need for advance preparation, then gathered the required tools as I surveyed the job ahead. Suddenly it occurred to me I might need some help.

Trouble is, my mate and I don't work well together. Unlike the perky couple on *Home Time*, who smile as they install kitchen cabinets, our projects often lead to a brawl. If *we* had a show, it would be called *Jail Time*.

Fortunately, after eighteen years of marriage, my groom knows this as well as I. "Don't be upset," he said, "but I'm taking over from here."

I objected ever so weakly and skipped off to do other chores. Two hours later, I returned to a bright, shiny basin.

"Well, what do you think?" Dan asked.

"You missed a spot."

He gave me "the look," but swept over the area with his brush.

"Bea-*utiful*!" I cried. "I'll get the bubble bath."

"Not so fast," he said. "This stuff takes three days to cure."

"Cure? Our tub has a disease? Don't tell me—lemme guess. Ringworm! Get it? Bathtub *ring*."

Dan ignored my joke and put away his tools. Thus began our seventy-two-hour wait to bathe. Every so often we'd sneak in to admire the fixture and get high on its fumes, but showering was strictly off limits. This produced a whole '*nother* set of fumes that rivaled fish and visitors combined.

But the moment finally came to try out our new porcelain pool. And we're all breathing much easier now.

DING DONG, THE SWITCH IS DEAD

WE ADDED A "NOTE"-ABLE improvement to our abode recently. No longer must visitors bloody their knuckles trying to get our attention—for now we have a (*Dong!*) doorbell.

We didn't always need one. Woody the Beagle used to howl good and loud when company arrived. When he passed away three years ago, so did our part-time doorman. Since then, I've stood like a sentry waiting for expected callers or risk missing their faint knock.

The practical one, my husband Dan studied a no-nonsense—read: cheap—doorbell kit at the hardware store.

"Let's get *this* one instead," I said eyeballing a more expensive model that played famous tunes. "I'd like to hear "Pomp and Circumstance" when someone darkens our door. Or, better yet, "Beethoven's Fifth." Bump-bump-bump *bom!* Bump-bump-bump *bom!*"

"Tell you what," Dan replied. "Let's save sixteen bucks and you can sing it yourself."

"It wouldn't have the same effect," I muttered.

Thus we hired an uninspired doorman for the low, low price of twelve-ninety-five. A wireless model, it installed in minutes, which is fortunate because Dan set it off a dozen times in the process. Instead of a majestic chime befitting a nearly-century-old home, it emits a tinny sounding din-dun—with the emphasis on din, if you catch my drift.

The novelty wore off after all of two rings.

But though it made its presence known during installation, it showed a temperamental side soon afterward, announcing callers on a rather sporadic basis. "Let's see," it seemed to say. "Do I *like* this person or not?" When it stopped working altogether, I changed my tune to Ding Dong, the Switch is Dead.

But I erred in that assumption. For those who haven't graced our home with a visit, let me give you a brief floor plan. Our front entryway is separated from the rest of the house by a heavy mahogany door. When closed, it creates a vacuum in the foyer that sucks beyond our Hoover's wildest dreams, but that's another story.

More to the point, it reduces the scope of our (*dong!*) doorbell. So we moved the receiver unit, which boasts a "one hundred-foot operating range," to a few scant yards from the dinger, and thus solved the problem.

Trouble is, now that our new (*dong!*) doorbell works right, no one comes to see us.

HEAR TODAY, GONE TOMORROW

OKAY, MAYBE IT was only earthshaking to *me*. But when I shared my heartfelt thoughts with my groom, he promptly changed the subject.

"You never listen to me," I said in a huff. (That's not exactly true, of course. Dan eavesdrops when I talk to myself, but the minute I address *him*, he squelches me out.)

"Sure, I do," he said defensively. "You were yakking about a sweater, right?"

"Wrong! It was a letter. A *rejection* letter."

He looked a bit sheepish so I moved in for the kill.

"You wouldn't pay attention to me if I stood on my head," I wailed, and stormed off to pout. But the visual reduced me to giggles instead. And it prompted me to think up some bizarre but effective ways we ladies might get through to our mates.

A police standoff, for instance. Picture this—dozens of cops surround the house, their squad car lights flashing. We discreetly slip out the door, seize their bullhorn and shout, "Now hear this! The grass needs mowing."

Or we might try hypnosis and put our spouses into a deep trance—not to be confused with lulling them to sleep, an all-too-frequent occurrence. Then, while his mind was relaxed and receptive, we'd fill it with all the news he'd normally blow off.

Jumping out of a cake may get some husbands' attention but, alas, mine is more of a pie man. Likewise, he wouldn't read an email even if it was marked "!" for priority.

But here's a thought. Next time my main man goes to buy an oil filter, I could hijack the store's PA system. "Attention K-Mart shopper! This is your wife speaking and we need to have a little chat."

Perhaps a vacation is the answer. We could drive to the Grand Canyon where I'd holler something of import. And if it didn't sink in after the eighteenth echo, I could give it another round.

For the husband who's passionate about pigskin, we wives could tackle their attention using one of several methods. Next time they go to a football game, we'd show up on the sidelines, shove a cheerleader aside, grab her megaphone and relay the desired message.

Or, in the money's-no-object department, we could buy a bazillion-dollar, thirty-second commercial slot for the Super Bowl game.

And hope he doesn't leave the room.

PLEASE DON'T SQUEEZE THE...

"LET'S SEE," I MUMBLED as I wrote out a shopping list. "Fish sticks...lunch meat..." My dear husband suddenly appeared so I sought his input. "What would you like that we haven't had in a while?" I asked.

"Sex."

"Very funny," I said. "I mean from the *store*."

"Well...how 'bout some—"

"Why do I even bother with a list," I interrupted. "I buy the same stuff every week."

Dan gave it another shot. "I could really go for some—"

"And there are too many choices," I griped. "It takes me half an hour just to get through the cereal aisle. Of course, that's partly due to defective carts that limp their way through the store—assuming I can extract one in the first place. Why do they weld them together like that anyway?"

"To save space," Dan replied. "Just yank 'em apart. I call that cart-us interruptus."

"Is that all guys think about?!"

"No. Sometimes we think about food—which reminds me...why don't you pick up some—"

"Then there's the meat that bleeds on everything in the buggy. Looks like a scene from *Psycho*."

"Ya know what I have a craving for—?" Dan tried once more.

"And after it's all said and done, I end up behind someone with a heaping cart and ten screaming kids."

"Why don't you just skip it this week?" said Dan. "We could live for a month on what's in the cupboard now anyway."

"Yeah, but we're out of bun wad."

"I see your point."

To my surprise, my Better Half offered to go, whereupon I spewed out umpteen reasons to the contrary. "For starters, it would cost twice as much."

"I'll bargain shop," Dan countered.

So with little fanfare, Dan deployed himself to the store, while I waited for my war-torn soldier to return from battle.

"So how did it go?" I asked, certain I'd hear a list of grievances.

"Fine."

"That's it?" I said. "Just 'fine?'"

"Okay, it went great," Dan replied as he headed for the door.

"Great?" I wailed. "What's great about shopping?"

Dan turned and smiled.

"The checkout girls."

WATTS WITH THAT?

HOW MANY CORCORANS does it take to change a light bulb? One—if he stands on stilts. The ceilings in this house are so high, I need scaffolding to reach them. Even my six-foot husband straddles furniture for the task. Why, I found footprints on the fridge the other day.

Trouble is, we go through more bulbs than Uncle Fester. Apparently none of us has learned the golden rule of light switches—what goes up must come down. Though only three people and a dysfunctional cat live here, there are times every bulb in the house is ablaze. In broad daylight even.

Clearly, we take Edison's invention for granted. Ever since its creation, a glowing bulb over someone's head has been the universal symbol for a brilliant thought. If that's the case, we should be approaching genius by now. So why do I have this moronic habit of turning the lights on as I'm leaving a room?

My husband, Dan, has his dim moments, too. Every morning I work out faithfully in the basement, and just as regularly he uses the bathroom down there. But once in a while, he shuts off the lights on his way up, leaving me to grope my way through the dark.

"Watts with that?" I asked one time after stumbling up the stairs.

"What's with what?" Dan replied.

"You turned off the lights on me. *Again*." This was no isolated incident, and I recounted several other times I had to make like Helen Keller.

"I forgot you were down there," said Dan.

"Excuse me?" I scoffed. "My ski machine sounds like a freight train roaring down the track. You mean to say you didn't *hear* it?"

To which he replied, "Oh, lighten up."

In his defense, at least he was conserving energy. Not *mine*, as it took me several hours to find my way. But electric energy, which is much pricier. In the same vein, he installed a crimson bulb in our bedroom to save money and—er—set a romantic tone.

"Fine," I said. "Just remember—red lights mean stop."

"I suppose you have a better idea?" Dan challenged.

"Sure do," I replied. "Why don't we install a motion detector light."

"In *this* room?" he quipped. "It would never go on."

MAY *NOT* CAUSE SIDE EFFECTS

EVERYTHING I SAID AGGRAVATED my Better Half that day and I finally confronted him. "Why are you so on edge today?"

"Because I took allergy medicine," he replied. "And the box says I may become irritable."

"No, you may *not*," I countered.

That's the trouble with taking drugs. They have this uncanny power of suggestion. Even if they don't induce the side effects listed, just knowing the potential exists makes us act the part.

That goes for medical conditions, too. Volumes of information on every known disease exist for those who need it. But they bring out the inner hypochondriac in the rest of us. ("Oh my gosh! Loss of appetite...increased pulse...I must have beriberi.")

Remember Wile E. Coyote, who never fell 'til he realized he was off the cliff? He proved that too much knowledge is a dangerous thing. To give you a more relevant example, whoever heard of the purple pill a few years ago? Most people suffering from old-fashioned heartburn took old-fashioned baking soda and that was that. But thanks to TV commercials, the entire universe would swear it has acid reflux.

Either that or erectile dysfunction. Have you seen the ad that's on now? An otherwise normal guy shows not a hint of humiliation as he states, "I get my Viagra with no wait, no embarrassment and..." Blah, blah, blah. He wears this matter-of-fact expression, as though discussing the weather. And a bright forecast at that.

Okay, it's not a drug, but the commercial for Serenity cracks me up, too. "The more you live..." says the voice over, "the more a bladder control issue shouldn't hold you back." And the camera pans this active gal through her busy day proving, beyond a doubt, that her threads stay dry. If viewers could judge the Emmy Awards, I'd vote that Number One.

But I digress.

Drugs have an additional drawback in that they're addictive. I was hooked on sleeping pills 'til it dawned on me they cause constipation. In the interests of decency, I won't expand on how I reached that conclusion. But I *will* say that our current Ex-Lax supply expired four years ago—which is *another* beef of mine.

So next time I can't sleep, I'll try something that may cause drowsiness. And once I conk out, Dan can become irritable all he wants.

SOMETHING TO WINE ABOUT

IT PROMISED TO be our best wine to date. We racked it more often—unlike prior batches, which were as clear and sparkling as swamp water.

Before I expand on this new and improved vino...a bit of history. You may recall that the one plant I never killed is a mulberry bush. Each summer I stoop to gather hundreds of fallen berries, the main ingredient for our recipe. This yields a sizable vat of cheap port, unless you count chiropractor fees.

Orson Welles knew the importance of time in making a great wine, but even rotgut like ours requires a waiting period. So I bided mine as I passed through our basement-cum-wine-cellar each day. Gradually I noticed the volume of our latest brew seemed to diminish and brought this to my Better Half's attention.

"We need to tighten the caps," I declared.

"Why is that?" asked Dan.

"Our wine is evaporating."

This was met with muffled snickers. In a matter of weeks our brew had vanished completely, but not before I siphoned a glass for myself. As anticipated, it tasted darn near tolerable. Drier than Death Valley, but a vast improvement over previous efforts.

This inspired us to want to produce more, but our mulberries were long gone. Luckily, one can make wine from all sorts of stuff—fruit, dandelions, gravel. No sooner did this happy thought occur to us than we came into a major apple windfall.

Dan rounded up the other ingredients. "How much sugar do we need?" he asked, holding a near-empty bag.

"Let's see," I said, hauling out the calculator, "If there are four-hundred-fifty-four teaspoons in *one* sack..."

He returned from the store long before I ciphered the answer.

"This should only take fifteen minutes," he announced as we began. Still peeling over an hour later, I pointed out his miscalculation.

"Stop griping or I'll give you something to 'wine' about," Dan quipped.

To core the fruit, my handyman husband sharpened a thin-walled pipe that worked better than the Real McCoy. (Doesn't that sound like a McDonalds food?) In lieu of a food processor, he used a two-by-four to crush the apples. Only he "wood" do something like that.

And to stir this bigger-than-average batch, Dan recruited a plunger. Nevertheless, I'm anxious to give it a taste. That is, if it doesn't evaporate.

(NOT) GETTING IT DONE

"YOU CAN GROW to hate that phrase," I muttered as I juggled a purse, some merchandise, and a walkie-talkie. My Better Half and I bought two-way radios to facilitate shopping, but all they encouraged was a headache.

Haunting the opposite end of the mall, Dan's voice crackled in the receiver. "Can you hear me now?" This he yelled for the tenth time in as many seconds.

My future purchase slid to the floor as I struggled to key the mike. "*Yes*," I hissed. "And so can the rest of the store!"

It seemed like a good idea at the time. TV ads show all manner of people getting it done with walkie-talkies these days. And they're more than just two-way radios. Any number of consenting adults can join in, provided they're on the right channel.

Thanks to a reducing diet, walkie-talkies have become slim little numbers the size of a small spud. When the price dropped along with their girth, we set out to buy what we viewed as cheap communication. Little did we realize they devour batteries like croutons at an all-you-can-eat.

The salesman showed us a variety of gadgets designed to make our lives easier. "This one reaches up to seven miles when you're on water."

Great, I thought. *I'll remember that next time we have a flood.*

"What does FRS stand for?" asked Dan.

"Family Radio Service," I said smugly, having just read it on the package. Turns out it *really* meant Face Reality Soon.

After making our purchase, we sat down on a bench to figure out how to use it. To give you an idea of the duration, a pair of mall walkers breezed past us no less than a dozen times. I glanced at my lengthy shopping list now and then.

I could get it done in the time it's taking to do this, I thought wryly.

With some last minute instructions, Dan sent me on my way. "I'll never lose her again," he said aloud, and a fellow patron overheard.

"Yeah," he agreed. "But now she can keep track of *you*, too."

Unless you count interference from every electronic device between Point A and Point B. Or the conversations of umpteen *other* shoppers who had the same moronic idea.

So when Dan suggests the two-way, I balk.

"How 'bout no-way."

THE "D" WORD

THIS NOVEMBER 24TH marks nineteen years of never-a-dull-marriage. In the mid-'80s, my hubby and I got hitched by a Justice of the "Peace"—a bit ironic when you consider all the bickering we do. If you read this column much, you know we have our share of tiffs, spats and all-out brawls. And though we'd rather fight than split, I'm ashamed to say the "D" Word has crept into the conversation now and then.

Luckily, a few things held us back, not the least of which was the cost. Comparatively speaking, divorce can be every bit as steep as the wedding that preceded it—and you have zip to show for it. No fancy duds...no shiny gifts...not even a caketop.

The retainer alone costs untold body parts even for uncontested divorces, but it's unlikely we'd find ourselves in agreement. We've debated every conceivable issue since tying the knot, including such vital concerns as which channel to watch. Add to that the matter of custody regarding our only child, Milo the Cat and the remote control—and you've got a hefty attorney tab.

That explains the rising popularity of online divorces. A number of web sites now exist that specialize in break-ups at a fraction of the cost of a live lawyer. For a flat fee of two-hundred-forty-nine bucks, Completecase.com generates the required court forms based on your answers to its highly personal questionnaire. In addition, it offers online support, which is not to be confused with life support.

The fees and services provided vary from site to site, but they all cover the two basic types:

(a) Divorce with minor children, and

(b) Divorce with spouses who *act* like minor children.

For the budget-minded bride, Mylawyer.com offers a generic divorce kit (good in all fifty states!) for a thrifty thirty-four-ninety-five . These are no-fault divorce kits but, if our union is any indication, there's plenty of blame to go around.

No-fault simply means neither party caused the breakup through cruelty, desertion or bed hopping. The only grounds needed to split up are irreconcilable differences. In that case, my checkbook and bank statement would qualify.

This is also referred to as irretrievable breakdown of the marriage. So far, my Better Half and I have always managed to retrieve it.

And keep the "D" Word at bay.

HOUDINI HUSBAND SYNDROME

DEAR NEW BRIDE,

You won't find it in your wedding planner, but there's something you should know. Chances are that attentive man you just married will morph into what I call a Houdini Husband. Many grooms feel a need to escape from time to time—as though marriage and prison are synonymous. If *they* planned the nuptials, wedding cakes would have files in them.

My Other Half spends four, maybe five, nights at home before feeling a deep need to skip town. Lucky for him we have a rustic camp to flee to when a shack attack (as he calls it) occurs.

"When will you be back?" I ask, so I'll know when to call the hospital.

"I *hate* that question," he mutters. Then in a more audible tone, I hear, "A couple of hours." In Houdini Husband talk, this means sometime after Groundhog's Day. Soon, only a puff of smoke remains as he drives off in his getaway truck.

When there's no time for an overnighter, Dan will announce, "I've gotta go lock up the garage." I've fallen for this line on countless occasions. He's on the lam for hours after this clever scam. Ten minutes later it dawns on me I've been duped.

I used to take it personally 'til I realized how common this trait is, though frequency and duration vary from guy to guy. Some are as habitual as my Main Man, while others are satisfied with an annual fishing trip. Houdini Husbands are the ones who come home empty-handed.

Some guys don't actually leave the premises, but escape via the Internet. "I'm gonna check my email," they say before launching themselves into cyberspace.

Still others use the buddy system. Dan's friends often phone and, in hushed tones, say, "Call me right back and say you need help with something."

Dan swiftly obliges by dialing his buddy's number. "Hey—insert friend's name! C'mon over—I need help with something!"

The friend then tells his wife, in all honesty, that Dan called needing assistance. Not being as gullible as I, she rolls her eyes and shows him the door.

So here's my advice to you, New Bride. Stifle the urge to use your groom's wedding photo for a wanted poster. Just enjoy the fact he's out of your hair.

And gimme a jingle.

Sincerely,

Aunt Corky

CHAPTER 2 – HAPPY HOLIDAZE

A RESOLUTION REVOLUTION

IT'S HARD TO forget that New Year's Day is right around the calendar. I can't turn a page without some know-it-all celebrity advising me of what resolutions to make. The latest wizard of Wall Street suggests I get a financial grip in the coming year. Kathy Ireland urges me to make still another fitness vow to hop 'til I drop.

The other day I read an article listing forty-some pledges I should make for a brighter New Year. As if I could remember them all long enough to keep them. "Enough!" I cried, and tossed it on the carpet I'd failed to vacuum. No one's gonna tell *me* what to resolve.

I grabbed a note pad and slid into thinking mode. Soon I came up with a list of off-the-beaten-path-but-a-cinch-to-keep promises, handpicked from my very own brain. In no particular order, they are as follows:

(a) Dine out more. By that, I mean Mexican food...Italian food...Chinese food. This will help me forge an ethnic bond with other nations as well as skate out of cooking. To say nothing of washing dishes.

(b) Stay up later. Frankly, I'm tired of pooping out at eight o'clock. I want to watch the ball drop in Times Square and not some after-the-fact video on *Good Morning America*. I want to stay up late *every* night and nap when I feel like it. In other words, I wanna be my cat.

(c) Waste more time on the computer. (Or, more accurately, *at* the computer. I'd hate to fall off again.) Never mind it would be spent deleting junk mail. As for *when* to do this, see (2) above.

(d) Save more stuff. The other day my son needed six toilet paper tubes for an engine he was building. Cylinders, don't ya know. In a matter of minutes I handed him half a dozen from my private collection. I hate to brag but how many parents could *do* that? So I want to stockpile even *more* things—in case he wants to erect a condo.

(e) Substitute bad habits for other bad habits. Even bad habits get old, so occasionally I'd like to explore new territory. Nailbiting... cracking my knuckles...that sort of thing.

And last, but most certainly not least,
(f) Stop reading celebrity advice columns.

DEAR DIARY OR BELOVED BLOG?

MY LIFE IS an open book. Actually it's *thirteen* open books if I break into my diaries all at once. I started journaling what seems like a century ago and can describe, in nauseating detail, the last forty-eight hundred days. These diaries are well hidden—not because they contain deep, dark secrets, but because snoopers would die of boredom and I would face murder charges.

I relish opening a brand spankin' new journal on January 1st each year and derive great satisfaction from writing the last entry. It's the pages in between that pose a problem.

There is little time for journaling during the week, so I jot down cryptic notes designed to jog my memory. And for an hour each weekend, I spill my guts in my dear diary before returning it to its secret shelter.

I understand this method of journaling has become obsolete, however. These days, book-type diaries are out and "blogging" is in. Yes, I know. It sounds like something folks do who drank too much, but the term is actually short for "web logging." Blogs are personal journals on that most public of places, the Internet.

Not surprisingly, they are interconnected so you can read other people's deep, dark secrets and they can access yours—if, in fact, you are crazy enough to publish them. Furthermore, you can comment on each other's writings. Dialogue ranges from supportive been-there type statements to what–are-ya-nuts? I can only imagine what remarks my mind-numbing entries would inspire.

Blogs are a fine forum for recording your hopes and dreams as well. What happens if you have no innermost thoughts? Or outermost either, for that matter? Dozens of journal prompts await you at www.exboard.com. Here's one: "If you could have a conversation with yourself, what would you say?" My question is, What do they mean by *if*?

www.blogger.com offers free blogging to the general public. Some sites are aimed more toward specific hobbies and interests. And still others, like iWorkwithFools.com, provide a place to vent. Sort of a World Wide water cooler.

Blogging speeds up what has traditionally been a tedious process. One can type in minutes an entry that would take half an hour to write in longhand. But, like the old method, it's therapeutic.

So start the New Year blogging. And drink plenty of fluids.

WRITE UNDER YOUR NOSE

I INVITE YOU TO celebrate National Handwriting Day on the 12th of this month. Or possibly the 23rd, seeing as some debate exists over when it occurs.

What the people who establish weird holidays *do* agree on is that it coincides with John Hancock's birthday. Why? Because, unless you're a *Jeopardy* contestant, his sprawling signature is the only one on the Declaration of Independence that you recall. ("I'll take Forgotten Americans for a hundred, Alex.")

This explains the connection between Hancock and Handwriting Day. However, if you research this on the Net, you'll find that the date of John's birth is *also* up for argument. One has to wonder if *he* even knew.

This is a big deal, folks. A man's astrological fate is at stake here. Imagine going through life reasonably certain of your Capricorn status. You unfold the *Colony Chronicle* to read your horoscope, and it says something like, "Now is the time to risk your entire fortune on a real estate venture." So you act on that advice and *then* find out you're an Aquarius.

Since no one is alive who knows for sure, we could simply host one long bash throughout mid-January. But to simplify matters, let's say Mr. Hancock made his debut on January 23rd. This is, in fact, the claim made by Writing Instrument Manufacturers Association, an organization with a bit of a stake in National Handwriting Day. Unless you enjoy scrawling in blood, you'll need a pen or two to participate.

Which brings me to the next question: how should one celebrate? And a dumb question that is. Nevertheless, I queried the Writing Instrument Manufacturers, who suggested organizing an essay contest. So your assignment, should you decide to accept it, is to hand write a four-hundred-word article on useless holidays.

If essays aren't your cup of ink, this suggestion is "write" under your nose: pen all of the day's correspondence in your finest script. This could mean letters to family or your friendly editor. Or practice your penmanship with rosters. For example, one might write a To Do List, a grocery list, or, depending on your relationship with co-workers, a hit list.

Perhaps you have time for only brief messages, but these should be neatly penned as well. There's no excuse for sloppiness on that ransom or suicide note. If nothing else, sign your name legibly.

Do it for John.

SNOW PAIN, SNOW GAIN

THE SURGEON GENERAL says fifteen minutes of shoveling counts as moderate physical activity. I always thought matters unrelated to smoking were beyond his jurisdiction. Nevertheless, when the Surgeon General talks, I listen.

So snow removal replaces my morning workout on a fairly regular basis now. It provides all the benefits of aerobic exercise without the leotards. And any dumbbell knows it involves weight lifting, too.

At least most of the time. Normally I sweep aside the first few snowfalls of the season with a broom—my way of pretending it's not really winter yet. When that device breaks in two, I graduate to a bona fide shovel, such as it is. You know how I hate to gripe, but ours leaves a ridge of snow in the center like an albino snake. Not the most efficient tool in the shed.

If *I* have my way, in fact, it's not in the shed at all. This is another area where my Better Half and I differ. I like to keep it close to the house so I don't have to trudge through drifts to retrieve it. Otherwise I get snow in my waders.

Shovel in hand, I vow to beat pedestrians outside. Not in the violent sense, although I'd like to at times. If I don't get there first, their feet pack the snow down, making my job more difficult. But I could start at midnight and still encounter people tracks.

Early winter finds me clearing a sidewalk-wide path down to the bare pavement. By season's end, however, it more closely resembles an Indian trail, and I could give a rat's rump how much snow lurks underneath.

This is partly because the snowbanks morph into a mountain range. And whatever I throw on Old Smokey trickles back down, or worse, causes an avalanche.

Because our methods differ, Dan recently gave me pointers on the proper way to shovel. Now that I follow protocol, it's become a totally mindless chore, freeing me to think any number of thoughts. Like how much I hate to shovel.

It's important to practice safe shoveling. A smaller shovel places less strain on your heart. In keeping with the aerobic idea, some authorities recommend warming up first. Therapist Noah Hyman advises, "Keep your back straight." Never shovel after eating or smoking. And dress appropriately.

Anything but spandex.

UP TO MY ELBOW GREASE

GRANTED, I'M A LITTLE late with spring cleaning, but I'm up to my elbow grease in it this week. You'd think a rent deposit was at stake.

I began this mission with the fridge, and found leftovers dating back to the late 1900s. After pitching them out, I turned my attention to taco sauce spills that gave the impression Jeffrey Dahmer lived here.

When DNA tests came back negative, I moved on to the stove. My oven cleaner's label recommended wearing hand and eye protection, so I changed into hockey gear and set to work.

The product certainly lived up to its name, easily taking the charred remains "off." Unfortunately, it took forever to *burn* "off," which caused the smoke alarm to *go* "off." Needless to say, that ticked *me* "off."

But after a good night's sleep, I resumed this venture and turned my attention to the cupboards. By now it had occurred to me that a little music might make the job more enjoyable. So I flicked on the radio and washed woodwork to the lively beat of commercials.

I had trouble reaching some of the nooks and crannies, but a toothbrush proved to be the right tool for the job. Don't tell him, but my husband Dan's was the perfect length. Unfortunately, it sprayed murky water all over, proving the theory that for every action, there is an equal and opposite reaction. The cleaner my cupboards became, the dirtier the Happy Housekeeper got.

My ten-year-old drifted in from time to time offering comic relief. "If you scrub too much," he said, "you're gonna get ammonia."

Too busy gagging, I made no reply.

"*Get* it?" he coaxed.

"More likely I'll get asphyxiated," I said, gasping for breath. I raced to the window and inhaled deeply. Thus I revived myself for the *other* half of the project, which is...

...to get organized. Luckily I remembered reading a nifty tip in Heloise What's-Her-Face's column. (See her Five-Point Plan at www.Heloise.com.) In a nutshell, to control clutter she advises something called the "Five Minutes or Five Things" Plan. Using this method, one can either concentrate on a job for five *minutes* or he/she can pick up, toss out or put away five *things*.

At that rate, it'll take me five *years* to spring clean.

DO YOU FOOL LIKE I DO?

IT WASN'T EASY finding good, clean pranks for my sixth annual April Fool's column. I found most of the jokes I scanned to be hilarious, but unprintable. But I persevered for my faithful readers and present the three of you with my results.

Achy Breaky Lark: Fashion a fake cast by cutting finger holes in a long white sock. Then slide it over a piece of cardboard you've curled around your arm. For added effect, write, "Get well soon!" on it.

Book 'Em, Danno: Buy a thick volume at a thrift store and carve a hole through the pages an inch from each edge. Then plant something smelly inside (limburger cheese, perhaps?) and place it on your mark's bookshelf.

Caller ID-iocy: If a telemarketer calls, pretend he or she is a long lost friend. ("Man, talk about a ghost from the past! So how've you been anyway?")

Car Caper: Pry off one of your stooge's hubcaps and insert a few marbles for some interesting sound effects.

Loony Tunes: Change the soothing 'hold' music on your office phone to heavy metal.

Mannequin Trainee: Draw a life-size face on a piece of cardboard and attach it to a broomstick. Then dress your dummy and prop it up in a closet your victim routinely uses.

Name That Goon: Swap the name plates of your co-workers.

Phone Farce: Call the people listed above and below your name in the phone book and tell them you just want to be neighborly.

Powder Play: Sprinkle some baby powder on your mark's bath

towel while he or she is in the shower.

Smashing Idea: Attach an anonymous note to someone's windshield reading, "I'm sorry I hit your car. Please call me so we can take care of this matter." (Don't leave a phone number, of course.) Your victim will spend a riotous amount of time searching for nonexistent damage.

Stuck on You: Write, "April Fool's" on one side of a snap-type clothespin and "From (your name)" on the other. Then clip it to your stooge's attire.

Tiptoe Through the Typos: Stuff the toes of your mark's shoes, boots or slippers with a wadded up newspaper page.

You've Got Junk Mail: Send advertising back in its postpaid envelope.

Water You Waiting For?: Tape the sink's spray hose so it remains engaged for the next unsuspecting user.

CHECKING YOUR FOOL GAUGE

THIS MARKS MY seventh annual April Fool's column, and I searched far and wide for a whole new pack of pranks. Ranging from comical to crazy, here are a gander of gags to play on friends, co-workers and the unsuspecting public.

Auto Antics: If your stooge's vehicle has air bags, blow up a white trash liner and tape it to the steering wheel.

Bathroom Brouhaha: Switch the Men and Women signs in public restrooms.

Computer Caper: Drive your victim crazy with fake error messages. Available as a free download from "www2.hawaii.edu/~rubio/error95/".

Doorway Deception: While your mark is sleeping, tape plastic wrap around a doorway he must pass through.

Juice-less Fruit: Unplug your stooge's appliances such as the stove, TV, etc. Note: Best to leave the fridge and iron lung alone.

Lottery Lark: Videotape the daily lottery drawing. Then buy your victim a ticket with the winning numbers and play back the tape.

Mail Mischief: Send your mark a letter with a joke return address, i.e. AIDS Testing Center.

Phony Phone Message: Leave your stooge a phone slip from Myra Mains with the number of a funeral home. (My remains...get it?)

Poster Prank: Use a computer to create a Wanted poster featuring your victim's mug, and post copies in various locations. Better yet, label it Unwanted.

Potty Plot: Set the rod in your mark's spring-loaded toilet paper dispenser a little off kilter.

Reading Ruse: If your stooge enjoys curling up with a good book, tuck an unlikely volume under the dust jacket of her current choice.

SARry Sight: Leave a stack of surgical masks at the entrance of a building. Then place a sign that says "Due to Infection Detection, masks must be worn. Signed: Public Health Department."

Shower Scheme: When your mark hops in the shower, replace his bath towel with a washcloth.

Telly Tactic: Dab white-out or shoe polish on the ear piece of your victim's phone and then place a call to him.

The Last Straw: Go out to lunch or for drinks with intended stooge. When she uses the restroom, heat the bottom end of her plastic straw with a lighter and squeeze it shut.

Tweeter Trick: Remove the cover from your mark's stereo (or computer) speakers and insert cotton.

Above all, be sure to check your fool gauge often. Or risk running out.

ANOTHER TAXING SITUATION

I EYEBALLED THE CHAOS in front of me: W-2s, 1099s and hundreds of dinky pay stubs. Piles of paper, with a capital P, and not a calculator to be found. Leafing through the 1040 instruction booklet, I saw faces of missing children and felt every bit as lost.

Then I remembered my sister-in-law's tip. She's a helpful sort, despite working for the Infernal Revenue Service. "Go to www.irs.gov," said she. "It lists sites that compute tax returns for *free*." My favorite word. In an instant, I logged on.

After making my selection, a textbox warned, "You are entering a secured area." I held my breath expecting to trigger an alarm and be dragged off to prison. But the site opened tranquilly with a young couple smiling in front of their laptop. Obviously they hadn't blown an hour searching for *their* Texas instrument.

Or maybe they opted for the obnoxious ad on the screen that said, "Click here to turn your computer into a calculator! Only $9.95!" Dozens of other plugs appeared throughout the ordeal, each designed to capitalize on my growing state of confusion.

Like an accountant, the site asks questions and uses the answers to prepare a return. After responding to each prompt, the words, Please wait...appear on the screen. They *mean* it, too. You could type the entire U.S. Tax Code—with one finger—in the time it takes to enter data.

At one point, it asked how much Advanced Child Tax Credit I received—like I can remember clear back to last summer. With great reluctance, I left the secured area to hunt down the dope and clawed my way back.

Then it urged me to determine what percentage of my home is used for business. Fact is, I wrestle with column ideas everywhere, whether I'm burning dinner or sweeping dust under the rug. So I responded, in complete honesty—one hundred percent.

No sooner did I print out the federal return when another ad appeared. "Complete your state return in less time than it takes to sharpen a pencil!" *Yeah right*, I thought pointedly. *Try in more time than it takes to grow graphite.*

But I stifled the sarcasm.

"Maybe later," I replied. "I don't wanna tax myself."

ADMINISTRATIVE WHAT'S-IT WEEK

HAVING RE-ENTERED THE work farce, I have a keen interest in Secretaries' Week, also known as Administrative Professionals' Week. (Or, in *my* case, Administrative Amateurs' Week.) Yes, folks, one day each week, I change into Super Secretary garb in the nearest phone booth and make my way to the office.

It's no easy feat being an Administrative What's-It. We are expected to conquer computers bent on crashing, and learn every new program that comes down the pica. Our keyboard speed must be phenomenal to produce those Get-this-out-today! projects that sit on the boss's desk for a month. (I hate to brag, but I can make eighty typos a minute.)

Furthermore, we must possess the necessary foot-ear-hand-eye coordination to transcribe our supervisors' dictation tapes. This means wading through all manner of throat clearings, belches and other bodily sound effects. Otherwise our letters would read:

"Testing! Testing! Dear Mr. Smith:

(*Ahem! Cough! Cough-em!*) It has come to my (*Burp!*) attention that (*Scratch-Scratch!*) your account is seriously (*Blat!*) past due."

We Administrative Professionals must also be cordial but efficient on the phone no matter how often the &*$% thing interrupts us. And we're expected to keep strictly confidential business matters strictly confidential—regardless of how juicy they are. Hence, the word "secret" in secretary. (Since "tarry" means "goof off," I take the last part of the word literally as well.)

At any rate, given our numerous burdens, I assumed Secretaries' Week was the brainchild of some disgruntled Girl Friday screaming for recognition. But, in fact, it was started by a nice guy named Harry Klemfuss back in 1952. Though its name has changed, it's still celebrated the third week of April by over three-point-nine million Administrative What's-its. Some employers give their hard-working, dedicated personnel flowers, candy or gift certificates. Others buy them lunch. And some actually give a *paid day off.*

Just for the record, the maddening habits I mentioned earlier are merely a cross-section of the numerous chiefs I've had in the past. In *no* way do they reflect my present boss, who asked to remain anonymous. Accordingly, I won't divulge who signs the paycheck when I "don" my secretarial hat to bring home the "bacon." However, I *will* say that he's a thoughtful, well-mannered, *generous* individual...

...who reads this column.

GARDEN PAR-TY!

JUST IN TIME for planting season, I learned about the legend of Isabella. It seems her brothers objected to her affair with someone named Lorenzo, so they lured him to a nice, secluded spot and bumped him off. His spirit visited Isabella in a dream and told of the nasty deed and where to find the body. Despite her grief, Isabella severed the head and buried it in a sizable urn. Then she added seeds and grew one luscious pot of basil.

Now I know what they mean by "planting the evidence." This also explains why my gardening attempts have proven fruitless: I used the wrong fertilizer.

Poor Lorenzo wasn't the only soul to improve a harvest. It's a known fact that the ancient Aztecs offered thousands of human sacrifices in order to grow good crops. (In light of this, the other word for farming should be hurt-iculture.)

The Aztecs may have had an awesome harvest, but I refuse to resort to homicide. Still, I need to do *something* differently. The plot we've nurtured for the past few years wouldn't know fresh produce if I tossed it a salad.

What it is, basically, is a glorified sandbox. 'Til now, its only real purpose in life has been as a cat latrine. We added Peat and other guys to enrich the soil to no avail.

But in the words of Napoleon (more or less) we have not yet begun to garden. I did my homework this spring and found some agricultural procedures sure to improve our odds.

And we'll stick with something easy, unlike one species I read about. The titanium is also known as the corpse plant because its blossoms smell like rotting flesh. Why anyone would want it to flower is beyond me, but I bet it could be coaxed with a recipe I unearthed. Rose tonic purports to make everything bloom. Among other ingredients, it contains three cups of dry red wine, which brings new meaning to the term garden party.

Speaking of spirits, beer also helps things grow, but which brand? My guess is Bud. R-R! Furthermore, houseplants dig whiskey, but too much makes them slur their weeds. The complete formulas can be found in the *Year 'Round Garden Magic Program*. (E-mail me for ordering info.)

Now if you'll excuse me (hic!), I'm hosting a flower fling...

WHEN THE GROWING GETS TOUGH

EVEN THE FAKE flowers on our front porch wilted last year. Normally, though, we limit gardening to the back yard so the neighbors don't laugh themselves silly. But at least we never give up. When the growing gets tough, the tough get help.

So I scanned, with interest, a seed catalog we received last month, which proved to be a real iris-opener. For one thing, I learned that not all dirt is created equal, and serious gardeners should invest in a soil test kit. Frankly, I'd hate to go that route unless it's graded on a curve.

It's a no-brainer operation, though, meaning we needn't have a PhD to test our pH. And if by chance it flunks, the company offers chemicals to cure it in an easy-to-apply formula. Or so says the catalog.

When I'm through playing mad scientist, I can plow ahead with fertilizer. This comes in a variety of forms, but chances are I'll opt for tablets. Then I can chisel on them some horticultural commandments. For example, Thou shalt not take the name of thy garden in vain.

With those preliminaries out of the way, I can get down to the business of actually growing things. In that regard, the catalog shows full-color photos of every veggie you can imagine, most of which look like they pump iron. To illustrate its massive size, the megaton cabbage is shown cradling a real live infant.

"Look, honey," I said to my husband, Dan. "They sell babies now."

It also offers heirloom squash, which has unlimited uses. One could hollow out a wing chair and, as the name implies, pass it down from one generation to the next. Rather than buy seeds, though, I'm saving them from the food we eat. Hence, we anticipate a bumper pineapple crop this year.

At least it can't fall victim to ground rot. That's what normally happens to my produce. Either that or it's plagued by locusts or something. But the catalog has remedies for them, too, offering fungicides, insecticides and a swarm of *other*-cides.

And in the presumptuous department, it sells industrial strength steamers to make the job of processing my bean harvest easier. All three of them.

Still, with this storehouse of products, I feel a can-do spirit emerging. So we'll give it another try and see what comes up.

KITTY CORNER

ACCORDING TO THE American Veterinary Medical Association, there are fifty-nine-point-one million cats in the U.S. From the looks of it, most of them hang around this neighborhood.

So I'm pleased that June has been designated National Adopt-A-Cat Month. Research shows you can reduce your risk of heart attack by owning a cat—unless you step on its tail, in which case you increase your chances.

You may recall we opened our hearts (and skin) to a fur ball named Marble. She quickly assumed her position in the Corcoran pecking order which, as luck would have it, was miles above me. To illustrate, she lay relaxing, belly up on the living room floor one day. Having just showered, my husband, Dan, mischievously tossed his underwear in her direction where it made a perfect descent, cloaking her in Fruit of the Loom. Incensed by this, Marble screeched, jumped up and promptly bit *me*.

But lately, Marble has been acting almost civil and I wondered if she was depressed or something. There are ways to tell if your cat has the blues, says Pam Johnson-Bennett, a feline psychiatrist who's published such clinical bestsellers as *Hiss and Tell* and *Twisted Whiskers*. Some key signs are a change in weight and grooming habits. Although our pussy was never much for primping, she did seem to have lost her trademark appetite.

"Marble seems kind of glum lately," I announced to Dan one day. "I think she needs a companion."

"Are you kidding?" said Dan. "Marble hisses at *pictures* of cats."

"That only happened *once*," I replied. "Besides, maybe having a boyfriend would bring out her warm side."

"She doesn't *have* a warm side."

Through a carefully executed campaign of bribes and threats, I convinced Dan to give it a try. Thus, we came to know Milo, the sweetest tomcat this side of heaven. Possessing all the qualities of a faithful pooch without the work, Milo's as mellow as Marble is manic.

But before I could introduce them, Marble let out a hiss that lasted some twenty-four hours. This prompted Dan to issue an ultimatum.

"You can have one cat and one husband or two cats and *no* husband."

"That's a tough one," I said. "Can I think it over?"

But like a good wife, I chose Door Number 1 and kept Marble and her many moods. I just hope they're not cat-ching.

THE OTHER "F" WORD

ACCORDING TO AN informal survey I conducted, most folks are completely unaware July is National Baked Bean Month. It seems that few people besides Van Camps' employees know enough to observe the extended holiday. So I'm urging both of my readers to share in a moment of quiet reflection before kicking off a festival that's sure to be a ripsnorter.

To help you celebrate, your local grocer stocks a number of competing brands, most of which, in my opinion, taste like wet sod.

For those who prefer a little more zing, I recommend a visit to southernfood.about.com, a web site that offers over fifty beannie recipes for every palate.

Filled with fiber and plenty of protein, beans enjoy the reputation of being a highly nutritious food. They'd be perfect if not for their rather potent side-effect. The Surgeon General should require labels warning consumers—or, rather, their loved ones—of the dire consequences of eating too many. Or do the humane thing and include a sample of Beano.

Flatulence has plagued humans since the beginning of time. To prevent gale force winds, ancient Chinese match lighters whipped up an elixir using anise seed. In fact, the versatile herb is still in use today for staving off the F-word. Orange peel and dandelion have been known to bring relief as well. But, thanks to recipegoldmine.com, I learned that two drops of peppermint oil in a half cup of cool water is the easiest formula for repressing raspberries.

It occurs to me that women must have concocted these remedies because the men I know have no desire whatsoever to tame a toot. On the contrary, they find them a welcome form of entertainment as well as an amusing topic of conversation. When male bonding occurs, the subject inevitably turns to air biscuits.

Now I don't mean to generalize here. I'm sure somewhere on this planet walks a man who doesn't bid Gullible Gertie to pull his finger. Or strive to perfect the One Cheek Sneak. Or rate his poot performance on a scale of one to ten based on volume, fragrance and duration. He just doesn't hang around *this* crowd.

And I doubt he'll embrace National Baked Bean Month like the rest of mankind. If they ever get wind of it.

I LOVE A PARADE...TO END

I LOVE THE FOURTH of July, from the morning parade to the late night fireworks—if I can stay conscious 'til then. Last year's parade lasted so long it ran *into* the late night fireworks.

For some reason, there were far more entries than usual. Certainly more antique cars chugged by than normal. Frankly, I resent that term, since many of them were *my* age.

In addition, dozens of guys felt no qualms whatsoever about riding their lawn tractors down main street. They putt-putted by happily, leaving gas fumes in their wake. And a record number of horses left the same thing in theirs.

More musical groups jumped on the bandwagon than in previous years, too, each as noteworthy as the one before it.

Then there were the politicians who smiled amiably despite a chronic illness that makes their hands shake. Even more peculiar was the staggering number of faithful supporters behind them. These mobs swelled into the hundreds and stretched as far as the ayes could see.

The good news is, long parades mean a good deal more loot. Numerous participants tossed out candy to an endless line of rugrats. If the kids played their cards right, they could seize enough to last 'til trick-or-treat.

Not what you'd call aggressive, my son initially lost out to more intense competition, so I felt compelled to coach him.

"Ya gotta stay focused, Kell. Keep your eye on the goal and hustle, hustle, hustle!"

This resulted in a respectable haul of goodies which I, as a responsible parent, distributed in an orderly fashion. "One for you...two for me..."

Merchants gave out other treats, too. I was thrilled when a local kennel doled out dog biscuits 'til I remembered I have a cat. But plenty of handouts were more practical. Some groups passed out football schedules while others gave flags, coupons or beach balls. It was easy to get carried away in the free-for-all. I heard a guy behind me yell, "Throw me a Seadoo!"

But all good things must come to an end. Eventually the excitement died down and the last float faded off into the sunset. This occurred late last week or so I'm told.

Just in time for this year's parade to start.

A CAT-ASTROPHIC HOME BUSINESS

IN CASE YOU didn't know, August is Home Business Month. I consider this weekly column a home business because,

  (a) I write it from *home*, and

  (b) I give people the *business*.

It's crucial for us residential tycoons to set aside certain hours to work each day. Mine happen to be from four to six in the morning. Unfortunately, that's prime time for Marble the cat. To make matters worse, we've shared the same quarters for three vexing years.

I could always tell when she'd taken a midnight stroll across my desk from the cat hair clinging to the keyboard. But she didn't stop there. She roamed over the scanner and past the fax machine before parking her ample rump on my copier.

Her tail would twitch as she studied documents emerging from the printer like long, flat mice from a mouse hole. Often, after calculating her odds, she'd ambush them, and I'd have to toss their mangled bodies in the trash.

I wasn't crazy about housing her litter box in my office either. Somehow gravel mysteriously migrated to the far corners of the room. Like, was she digging for relics or what? I heard that cat lovers in this country bought one-point-eight million *tons* of litter last year, and I'd venture to say most of it wound up on my floor.

My biggest beef, however, involved her interruptions. The only raw material a writer possesses is ideas, but they vanish, never to be seen again, when I'm abruptly disturbed.

Picture this, if you will. Marble's snuggled on her makeshift bed with eyes shut, lulled by the sound of my typing. Nice, peaceful scene. A brilliant thought enters my head, and I fail to notice the brat cat awaken and stretch. Suddenly, she chooses this crucial moment to sharpen her claws on my steno chair.

Or she spies a ball of paper I crumpled up in frustration—one of many, I might add—and feels a deep need to pounce on it. Either way, my clever notion goes right through the shredder.

After years of frustration, it occurred to me to move her earthly possessions. So last week I relocated her food dish and litter box across the hall. She doesn't much care for the change, but my trusty squirt gun prevents her from returning.

And now she can no longer give *me* the business.

SIGNS OF THE PRIMES

FROM A GANDER AT the political signs around town, there are more people campaigning for office than there are voters. I'd run, too, but I hate to overexert myself.

Besides, I'd feel silly seeing my name in twelve-inch letters marring someone's landscape. Bad enough that it shows up in graffiti. Come to think of it, I could just edit what's there. ("For a good time, vote for...")

I have a real beef with political signs anyway. From a distance, they look too much like yard sale notices. The fluorescent colors grab my attention and visions of bargains dance in my head. Then I race down the street, only to suffer grave disappointment.

Interestingly, some yards support several different candidates for the same office. This means one of two things: either the resident is bipolar or has a marriage like mine wherein the parties never agree.

But signs aren't the only sign of the primes. The candidates themselves greet me cheerfully like old pals, pay me house calls and even buy me drinks. I'm a little confused though. Prior to the campaign, these sociable folks never gave me the time of day. While I enjoy the attention, I'm tempted to ask, "How come you weren't this friendly *before*?"

The phone offers another clue that this is election year. I reluctantly participated in a political poll the other day. The inquiring mind took twenty-odd minutes to ask me "a few" questions. Toward the end, she got pretty personal. "And would you describe yourself as very left wing, moderately left wing, moderately right wing or very right wing?"

"None of the above," I replied. "I'm more a tail feathers kind of person."

Which explains why I don't run for office. Besides, a lot of work is involved just getting my name on the ballot. Election forms must be completed and candidates must obtain "x" number of John Hancocks to qualify. (I wonder how many signatures John Hancock had to get.)

And that's just the beginning. After that, there'd be speeches to give and interviews to grant—a real stretch for a low-profile person like myself. And let us not forget the yard signs.

No, when it comes to public office, the only run I'd make is running for cover. Or maybe running amok. But first I'd want a running start.

GIMME A "B"REAK

FRESH FROM CAMP, the team lines up on the field. Regardless of their position, they'll all receive a pass. Or at least *most* cheerleaders do.

I have a confession to make. I've wanted to be one ever since my first pack of Old Maid cards. But I was way too shy to try out. *What chance do I have*, I thought, *to be one of the chosen few?* Turns out I was just born too soon. Cheerleading teams have grown by leaps and bounds over the years. (Get it?) Now they're the size of a chorus line.

I spotted swarms of them at a basketball game I attended last season. They easily outnumbered fans two to one. Their routines were quite a bit more daring than I remembered, too. I held my breath as they formed a formidable human pyramid. Then the girl on the third floor did a free fall into her teammates' arms and lived to tell about it. Personally, I'd opt for the elevator.

As I recall, the prehistoric cheerleaders in my day worked the crowd into a frenzy using sheer lung power. They also taught us how to spell. "Gimme a B...!" Often a random leg would spring up when the team scored and they executed their jumps as if the hardwood floor housed a trampoline. The real showstopper occurred when someone did the splits. And had the wherewithal to right herself before the players returned.

But all of that was small potatoes compared to today's routines. Besides the gravity defying stunt I spoke of, they've added gymnastics and choreography. The halftime show I saw focused almost entirely on the girls' dance skills, acrobatics and underwear.

Which brings me to a personal question: What's with *that* anyway? Is it really necessary to give the audience a free shot? My jaw hung open and my eyebrows refused to light as I took in the show. I wanted to yell, "Put yo' legs togetha, ladies!" Or maybe, "Gimme a 'B'reak."

That observation aside, the show featured a very talented bunch. From their synchronized movements, it was obvious they spent considerable time practicing. As Queen of Uncoordination, I was impressed to no end.

But that other part—the part that makes parents and innocent by-sitters blush—that's really gotta go, team, go.

HALF EMPTY OR HALF-WIT?

I HAD THE NICEST chat with a friend the other day. She's one of those don't-worry-be-happy kind of people. Despite her share of hardship, she still treats each moment as though school just got out.

I admire eternal optimists while, at the same time, being mildly irritated by them. This is because I'm an eternal pessimist. Let's say I won the lottery and am on my way to pick up the loot. Rather than focus on my outstanding good fortune, I would likely dwell on how much more tax I have to pay.

This comes from years of conditioning. When I awaken each morning, the first thought that pops into my head is routinely a worry. Recent notions include, Are my hubby and I still bickering or did we make up? And the ever popular, Why did I blow my diet last night?

Once I've worked this thought into a personal crisis, I rise and get on with the day—toting the anxiety along for the ride. To quote a pal of mine, "I need a U-haul to carry my emotional baggage."

Don't ask if the glass is half full or half empty. I'd just poke fun at the half-*wit* who came up with that analogy. But where did this brooding persona come from? It's not like I've been a prisoner of war or anything. At least not to my recollection.

In fact, I once was more like Pollyanna, the little girl who always looked on the bright side. She started fading when a classmate put me down for smiling too much. Gradually, the School of Hard Knocks wrung the life out of her and she reincarnated as Oscar the Grouch.

But it's high time she made a comeback. And what better day than September 13th, which some bozo dubbed Positive Thinking Day. How can cranks like me participate? There are a number of ways, according to Philip E. Humbert, Ph.D.

(a) Lincoln said, "Most folks are about as happy as they make up their minds to be." So we pessimists need to grab some pompons and be our own cheerleader.

(b) If it weren't for bad news, there'd be no news at all. Translated, that means do yourself a favor and skip Dan Rather.

(c) Be grateful for everything—even hokey holidays like Positive Thinking Day. And give thanks that they only last twenty-four hours.

A BUICK NAMED SUE

SINCE FEW VEHICLES have their own moniker, it's safe to assume not many folks observe Name Your Car Day. The little known American holiday, occurring October 2nd, should be celebrated by every licensed driver. Why?

Do you want your car conking out while crossing the highway? Of course not. Or making embarrassing noises in a crowded parking lot? No way! If you expect your vehicle to cooperate, you must treat it with respect. And what better way than to give it an identity?

As a public service, I dedicate this column to helping you name your Nissan, dub your Dodge, or christen your Chrysler, taking into account its unique personality. You can either inspect it first to determine gender, or play it safe with a unisex name like Bob.

Other plain but acceptable titles include Joe or Mary, but consulting a book of names will expose you to hundreds more creative handles for your pride and joy. *The Best Baby Name Book* (Bruce Lansky, author) is a handy reference that also lists the most popular foreign names—in case you have one of those imported models. But while Mohammed or "Françoise" may float your boat, I don't recommend Ping or Yuk.

A web site I happened upon offers a rather unique service for selecting a name. Just type in two others and BabyNameScramble.com will shuffle the letters to generate a list of monikers. This assumes you know your car's parentage, of course.

Since most people aren't privy to that info, one could base the name on specific characteristics. For example, we named our car Rusty. You may also recall reading about our van, which had a tendency to lunge forward on takeoff. Thus we called him Lurch.

Or let the letters on your license plate inspire you. TRU may stand for an aristocratic name like Thurston R. Urick (or Toys 'R Us).

The vehicle's color may also prompt an alias. I'm reminded of a friend who asked my advice in naming his Harley. Using my trusty computer, I printed out a list of dozens of things that are white, and narrowed it down to one. But he soundly rejected Snowball.

I guess I see his point. We don't want other vehicles making fun of our wheels and must keep that in mind when naming them.

Because life ain't easy for a Buick named Sue.

MAY THE VERSE BE WITH YOU

MARK YOUR CALENDARS because National Poetry Day falls on October 7th this year. Few people realize that, before becoming an obscure columnist, I wrote obscure poetry. In fact, I penned hundreds of poems, all of which reeked. This put me in a distinct minority because most awful poets have no idea they stink.

Part of the problem is many of us prefer poetry that rhymes. If it don't rhyme then, by gum, it ain't a poem. So we rearrange nouns and verbs to achieve this, but doing so does not a good poem make.

Or we leave things in the proper order, then search far and wide for words that sound the same. ("Hey, hon—what rhymes with Argentina?")

As a rule, poetically inclined persons tend to ramble, too. I have nothing against Henry Wadsworth Longfellow but let's face it—he wrote some pretty wordy stuff. I could see "Song of Hiawatha" condensed into two or three verses, tops. Someone should have introduced that guy to Haiku. Even his *name* could stand some downsizing.

Furthermore (and I exclude dirty limericks here), poems are often terribly depressing. That is, when you can understand them. I've read a variety of poetry over the years and too often my gut reaction was, "Huh?" For the sake of us dense readers, poets should just spit out the message and forgo the murky symbolism.

So it's small wonder some newspapers have banned poetry. But even institutions that *encourage* rhymes don't like mine. I sent dozens of verses to greeting card companies but, like homing pigeons, the sons of guns came back. Even my most poignant birthday salute was rejected.

"Roses are red
Violets are blue
Just a reminder—
I'm younger than you."

So you can imagine my delight when I received an invitation to this year's International Society of Poets Convention. Over eighteen-hundred patsies—er, poets—were to attend. Highlighting the prestigious event, a "professional poetry reader" was to recite each of our touching tributes—presumably with a straight face.

I toyed with the idea for the better part of five seconds before declining. "No thanks," I wrote back. "I'd have to part with my appendages to finance it and, gosh, I really hate crowds. I'll pass on the hundred-sixty-nine dollar custom-engraved Silver Award Bowl, too. But, hey, thanks for thinking of me.

And may the verse with you."

GOING IN-TOG-NEATO

IN KEEPING WITH the Potter craze, half a million Harrys went trick-or-treating last year, and my son was no exception. Cloaked in a black robe, Kelly beamed when people acknowledged his alter ego. But his smile faded when some bozo asked, "Are you running for judge?"

I wanted to wield the magic wand and yell, "Hey, buddy, does this look like a gavel to you?" Better yet, turn the offender into a toad.

He could have been joking but, then again, some folks don't recognize obvious costumes—like the time I wore a white sheet over my head to a party. Guests thought I was a bed.

That never dimmed my enthusiasm for Halloween, though, and I eagerly look forward to the holiday. A friend marveled at how I make my son's costume every year. A regular Martha Stewart, she called me. Too bad it takes 'til halfway through trick-or-treat to finish. ("Hold still, Kell! Just one more button to sew on...")

Though props lend a bit of authenticity to costumes, they should be avoided as the novelty quickly wears off. Children soon tire of carrying a stone tablet etched with the Ten Commandments. Chances are, Mom or Dad will have to lug it from door to door 'til a trash can presents itself.

Likewise, one should choose costumes that do not confine. I dressed as a pencil one year and had a devil of a time sitting down. Darn eraser. And since my vision was impaired, it was hard to get the lead out.

For those who prefer ready-made threads, www.hollywood-costumes.com hawks everything from cartoon characters to theater garb. Though not cheap, it offers plenty of novel ways to go in-tog-neato. Those wanting to be dressed to kill can even order Freddy Kruger duds.

The web site also sells harem getups for those gals who wear only provocative costumes. That's a real pet peeve of mine. C'mon, ladies! This ain't no beauty contest, so ditch the lipstick. Besides, Halloween is for reviving the little kid in all of us. Heaven knows life holds its share of stress, so if we can trade places with Daffy Duck for a while, then by gum we should do it.

Or join the ranks of Harry Potter clones. And be judge for a day.

A LEAF OF ABSENCE

I HAVE A LOVE-HATE relationship with our maple tree. It warms my heart to see it bud in spring and grow a lush blanket of leaves. And I marvel at the brilliant shades of red in autumn. It's when the sons-of-guns start falling that my devotion wears off.

I look at raking as an annual chore. That means *once* a year—not each time a breeze kicks up. Since our tree is the last to lose its leaves, we wait 'til the cows come home to start. And being good hosts, we let them shower and relax first.

For some reason, despite fierce autumn winds, at least one stubborn leaf clings to the tree. How dare it defy custom like that? So we wait it out a bit, stifling the urge to climb up and sever it with a machete. Finally we give up and head out in subzero temperatures.

This system does little for our neighbors, who, weeks before rid their yards of leaves—*our* leaves—only to have millions more blow back in. Clearly, we need to synchronize our lawn maintenance.

Is there a rake alive without bent tines? These provide an escape hatch for wayward leaves. Those that don't elude me end up hopelessly stuck in the implement. I spend more time dislodging them than I do raking. Why then do I end up with third-degree blisters?

Probably because we rake more than necessary. Each year we make a leaf house for our son, Kelly. To the naked eye, it appears to be nothing more than a crooked floor plan. With a little imagination, however, it becomes a spacious abode with full bath and roomy master bedroom. But no sooner is it finished and someone suggests a remodeling job.

"Why not gut it and build a condo," I quip. "What is this, keep up with the Joneses?"

My timing stinks, too. Often I see the official city leaf-picker-upper drive by as I toil, but it does a Houdini the minute I deposit my load at the curb.

We *could* fill leaf bags, but it takes us 'til spring to toss them out. Speaking of which, it makes more sense to rake during that season. Leaves are soggy and more apt to stay put, so I vote we do it then.

And take a leaf of absence this fall.

TAMING HOLIDAY RAGE

HERE'S A POP QUIZ for you. November 29th marks the start of *which* annual season? How many guessed Christmas shopping? Wrong. It ushers in four weeks of Holiday Rage—the period when your average, well-adjusted family is most likely to go berserk.

Having been there and done that, I wouldn't set foot in a store the day after Thanksgiving for fear of amputation. If I was lucky enough to retain my limbs, I'd be trampled by a crowd of frenzied shoppers in search of Rapunzel Barbie.

Assuming I survived the trauma, I'd hobble to a checkout line that snakes out the door and into the next zip code. Weeks later, I'd return to my family a drooling vegetable that mutters, "There's no place like home."

But shopping is only one factor that contributes to Holiday Rage. We can also count on heated debates with our mates over issues like money. ("You paid *how* much for that gift?") And whether or not to send Christmas cards in light of postage rates. ("They should replace the soaring eagle on mail trucks with a flying dollar bill.")

Furthermore, we argue over which activities besides shopping, baking and wrapping to pack into a few scant weeks. Like the Santa parade. ("Reruns already?") And assorted holiday parties. ("Does this lamp shade make me look fat?")

We also dicker over whether to decorate outdoors. Should we procrastinate 'til it's too late (as usual)? Or compete with the Joneses, whose house looks like Liberace's closet.

So there's plenty of Christmas cheer to stress out over. And when you cram it all together, you have a classic case of Holiday Rage. The secret is to nip tension in the bud before it reaches the homicide stage. How do we do that?

At the risk of dating myself—how does one *do* that anyway?— I've learned how to cope from an old episode of *My Three Sons*. When nice guy Steve Douglas was deeply upset—and you could tell because his smile wasn't as wide—he'd go for a walk to cool down. By the time he returned, he (and the show's writers) knew the perfect lines to restore harmony.

So that's what I plan to do this holiday season. Northern winters being what they are, it shouldn't take me long to cool off.

I just hope I don't slip on a patch of ice.

BLOWING HOT AND COLD

IN CASE YOUR goose bumps failed to tip you off, be advised that winter begins December 22nd. It's no small coincidence it's also

Thermometer Day. Before the advent of this device, folks measured sub-zero temps by how fast their teeth chattered.

Though Daniel Fahrenheit didn't invent thermometers, he was the first to make two that gave identical readings—which is more than I can say for mine. The early gauges used alcohol, but subsequently went on the wagon.

Needless to say (but I'll type it anyhow), thermometers have come a long way since then. Tired of measuring the Big Chill, these gizmos have wormed their way into warmer locales like the kitchen. They can be found regulating such appliances as ovens and microwaves. And meat thermometers tell us when our roast is running a fever.

Which reminds me... There are a variety of ways to take one's body temperature these days. It used to be oral thermometers were all the rage, but now we can monitor that sort of thing through the ear. The one I studied for this column resembled a chunky phone receiver. It gives accurate readings with no discomfort whatsoever—unless mistaken for a rectal.

Digital thermometers have their flaws, though. I endured a record-breaking hot flash the other night and, on a whim, decided to measure it. So I dashed downstairs, careened around the corner, and halted in front of the medicine chest. There I made out with our high-tech thermometer only to find the battery had died.

Furthermore, digitals allow no opportunity to fudge. In the good ol' days, there was a certain satisfaction in watching that mercury rise. ("See that? I *am* sick.") And if it failed to shoot high enough, one could apply nail polish for added sympathy.

I'm not the only one who prefers traditional thermometers. Organizations often use giant fake ones to show their fund-raising progress. And while researching this column, I ran across a rather novel application.

At SexThermometer.com, one can type in the names of two people and push a button to measure their compatibility. To test the theory, I paired myself with a few celebrities. No chemistry existed between Tom Cruise and me—at least not on *his* part—but Godzilla and I were quite an item.

So I may spend Thermometer Day with him.

SINGING THE BOX OFFICE BLUES

HAVE YOU HEARD of Operation Christmas Child? Participants fill shoeboxes with toys and small items for a designated age group. The presents are then distributed to hungry children in poverty-stricken countries. You can imagine how their faces light up—before devouring their gift, cardboard and all.

It being a worthy cause, I decided to participate this year, so I hiked up to the attic where our boxes reside. Actually, that's an understatement. They have, in fact, seized control of the area and ambush those brave enough to venture north. Fully three-fourths of the attic consists of empty parcels of various sizes. Since it also shelters a mean supply of bubble wrap, you'd swear a UPS truck exploded up there.

It all started when my son was in preschool. I bought him a book called *Build it with Boxes* (Joan Irvine, author) and from that point on, cardboard provided the raw material for all manner of entertainment. Cartons that had led a boring existence storing soup cans, for instance, reincarnated as race cars, boats or whatever else Kelly had a hankering for.

Thus was born a Save-the-Boxes obsession. Whether it held teeny, tiny earrings or massive major appliances, it claimed a spot in our box office. More than once I saved one from certain death.

"Stop!" I'd shout at my husband, Dan, poised to demolish a perfect specimen.

"I'm just recycling it," he'd reply defensively.

"I'll recycle it my own way, thanks," I'd say.

Then I'd haul it away to join the others. The only one missing was Pandora's Box, which, in reality, describes the attic. You don't *even* wanna go up there.

With an inventory like that, you'd think I'd have a box for any occasion. But truth is, I can never find the right size. Being cheap, I hate to use more gift wrap than necessary, so I spend days searching for one with the proper dimensions. When I *do* uncover it, it sports puncture holes from Kelly's abandoned projects.

And so it went with Operation Christmas Child. Try as I might, I couldn't find a shoebox to save my life. So I did what any self-respecting benefactor would do: I bought a pair of shoes. And I hope whoever gets them will savor them.

Along with the antacid I threw in. Just in case.

CHRISTMAS HANG-UPS

CHRISTMAS TREE ORNAMENTS often tell a story, but ours could produce a movie—provided it's a comedy.

The first "ornament" we attach is the colorful manufacturer's tag that came with our coulda-sworn-it's-real fake tree. It had a hole punched in the top and a string threaded through. (The card, not the tree.) Our son, Kelly, hung it for a joke one year and we've been adding it ever since.

Some ornaments mark his obsessions over the years. If one looks closely, he will spot Teletubbies, a Pokemon character and other remains of short-lived fads. (Thank heaven.) Others reflect our individual passions like fishing, sewing, and a computer that never needs rebooting. There's even a pinball machine that lights up and makes authentic noises. Something like my brother.

Photo ornaments from various ages portray our family history. Studying each one, I see how much Kelly has grown from year to year. And how much I've shrunk.

We have a number of personalized ornaments, too—little tokens with our names engraved in case we ever get amnesia. Ah, yes, now I remember. My name is Hallmark...

You'll glimpse candy canes and ornaments made from bread dough or macaroni that are well past their expiration dates. So eat at your own risk. We also have hang-ups derived from unusual materials like light bulbs and clothespins. Or more natural substances like Styrofoam.

Raise your hand if you *don't* have a Styrofoam ball with a name sequined on it. Those things last forever! The one I made in grammar school still looks new despite all the times it fell on its head.

Fabric ornaments aren't quite as indestructible. Woody the Beagle sank his canines into a few felt ones that were blinded by the incident. He also had a taste for wooden ornaments. As a result, our soldiers look like they saw one too many battles.

Marble the Cat is more interested in ornaments that smell—like the cinnamon sticks cleverly designed to look like fireplace logs.

Speaking of which, I've been meaning to start an *ornament* log. I got that tip from a woman's magazine a few years back, but still haven't gotten around to it. The idea is to include a description of each ornament and record from whence it came. That way I don't have to rely on my memory.

Now if I can just recall where I stored them...

HOW TO DRESS FOR STRESS

EVERYONE I MET FLASHED me a smile and I returned from my walk in high spirits. Even my husband, Dan, greeted me with a grin.

"Did you know your shirt is inside out?" He laughed.

"You're joking, right?"

Turns out he wasn't. I didn't need a mirror to see that seams formed prominent ridges down the sides and across my shoulders. And a non-designer label jutted out the back.

When it comes to clothing, I'm a few cedars short of a closet. You name the occasion, and I'll pick the wrong thing to wear—or the wrong way to wear it. Forget success. The way I dress causes nothing but stress.

To give you an example of my keen lack of timing, I scrapped a swell pair of twenty-five-year-old bell bottoms weeks before they came back into style. I'd replace them, if not for the high cost of fashion. Clothing stores are *so* pricey these days. They must think their shifts are good to eat.

Furthermore, I should have studied fashion terminology as a second language. I'm a bit fuzzy as to definitions and need a translator on the rare occasions I shop. She answers all of my chic-challenged queries like, what the heck is a weskit? Do two sarongs ever make a right? How often should one take a basque? And can a ruff ever be smooth?

For these reasons, I tend to stick with my current wardrobe. Trouble is, it's got its own problems. If the bust is the right size, it's too snug in the hips. And if the hips fit okay, there's room at the top for a Siamese twin. As a result, sleeves and straps tend to inch their way down. I either have to yank them back up or suffer an out-of-bodice experience.

Either that or the outfit fits great 'til I wash it or, more accurately, *dry* it. Then it shrinks to such dainty proportions even Barbie couldn't squeeze into it. Rather than throw it out, I let it hang in my closet, taunting me. Or worse, I opt for the sausage look and hold my breath all evening.

At least 'til I get home. "I'm gonna go slip into something more comfortable," I say to Dan, who likes the sound of that.

Then I come out in sweatpants.

LOSING MY DAY JOB

OUT OF THE blue a former boss called and asked if I'd come in for a day. "Sure," I said because,
    (a) I felt charitable, and
    (b) my bank account was severely depleted.
Besides, I thought it would be novel to play Miss Career Girl again.

I hung up the phone and stopped to reminisce for a moment. Though I've retired from the nine-to-five scene, I once took great pride in my job as a legal secretary. My reverie saw me type briefs faster than a speeding printer and leap tall file cabinets in a single bound. And that was *before* the morning coffee break.

So I oozed confidence when I showed up that day in my newly pressed superhero cape. The Head Boss and Chief Paycheck Signer briefed me on protocol before retiring to his office. Moments later, all heck broke loose.

The phone rang and I stammered my way through a greeting. I should have made a cue card because my mind drew a blank each time I picked up the receiver. ("Good morning! Attorney Ah...er...um... Just a minute, I'll think of it.") I couldn't say who was on the line or what they wanted—I was too busy trying to figure out the intercom. When that failed, I strolled as casually as possible to the boss's office to announce calls.

I bristled a bit when he introduced me to clients as his "old" secretary. *If you don't mind, I prefer the word former,* I thought to myself. Still, I greeted them as graciously as possible considering I was shaking in my pumps.

The mail arrived and with it, another opportunity to mess up. Make that two. I fumbled for ten-odd minutes with the date stamp, smearing ink on everything I pawed in the process. Then with a swift, final motion, I sliced the letterhead off correspondence I opened. The tape I used to reattach it revealed a distinct set of fingerprints.

The rest of the day went every bit as well, but somehow I made it through without destroying a single piece of equipment. And my boss seemed grateful for what he termed a "warm body" to keep things running. Never mind I had head-to-toe goose bumps from the air conditioning.

"Hey, I'll fill in any time!" I said as I waved goodbye.
Strangely enough, he hasn't called since.

THOUGHTS FROM A TYPO-WRITER

WHEN I LEARNED TO type three decades ago, I had no idea how many snickers could result from the skill (or lack thereof). I wish I'd had the foresight to save the typos I've seen since then. Fortunately, with us smack dab in the Keyboard Age, bloopers are more prevalent than ever.

The email my sister and I exchange, for instance, often results in some real gems. I laughed myself silly when she shared her recipe for "swill" steak, which is apparently like Swiss steak, only juicier. Thanks to a transposition, she said she felt "tried" from working all day. Or perhaps it was because she didn't "sleet" well the night before.

To accommodate his interest in computers, my son, Kelly, learned keyboarding a few years ago. He now types forty-five error-free words a minute. But every so often he makes a faux pas—like the report he wrote on the Revolutionary "Was."

Newspapers provide a constant source of mirth. Writer Richard Lederer is credited with spotting this head-scratcher: "...Kinney plans to increase the number of uninformed sergeants by fourteen..." And columnist Poke McHenry tells of a veteran cop who became irate when the press called him "Defective." To clear up the error, the paper printed an apology to Detective so-and-so from the police "farce."

Though less a typo than a brain boner, I still cackle over a For Sale ad I saw a few years back for a "chester drawers." I've heard of naming cars, but furniture??

Then there was the spam I received for a product similar to Viagra. "Dramatically enhances 'organism,'" it gushed. As if that wasn't enough to convince consumers, it claimed it would leave their partner gasping for "breadth."

But topping the Off-Color Department was an article my dad clipped ages ago from a now-defunct newspaper. The story described a "cookout" enjoyed by a group of Girl Scouts. But the typesetter inadvertently replaced the middle "o" with a "c," much to my father's amusement.

Perhaps you wonder why I've failed to include my *own* typos in this expose'. That is, of course, because I don't made any. As a legal

secretary for man years, I learnt the value of proof raiding. And that
talent serves me well as a weakly communist—er, kolumnist—er—
Righter.

CHAPTER 4 – HAVING A BAD HALO DAY

AGING IS GETTING OLD

I DISTINCTLY RECALL muttering some thirty years ago, "I can't
wait 'til I grow up." I had reasons for wanting to be older, though
they're a bit hazy now. Likely, they centered around the desire for
independence, a driver's license and abolishment of homework.

But now that I've had ample time to reflect, I've come to realize
adulthood isn't all it's cracked up to be. I merely traded in math
assignments for bill paying, checkbook balancing and tax return blues.
Independence, I've learned, is severely overrated. And I rarely
commute except to drive my husband crazy.

As anxious as I was to leave youth behind, I now miss most of its
benefits—number one being my metabolism. I'm not sure if it moved
out gradually or packed its bags and left in a huff. But there's little
doubt it's gone, with no chance of reconciliation.

I'd welcome my original hair color with open pores, too. Though
I can't recall the exact hue, *any* shade would beat the wiry gray hairs
that now spring out in all directions. It's also a great deal thinner than
before. I could build a nest for Big Bird with what gets trapped in the
drain plug each week.

I miss my former height, too. There was a time when I dismissed
five-feet-two as hopelessly dinky, but now it's an altitude I look up to.
Envy even. The Incredible Shrinking Woman has nothing over on me.

As a kid, I got a big bang out of wrinkling my forehead in the
mirror and watching it smooth out again. Now it impersonates a
washboard without any effort at all—and stays that way. Same goes for
laugh lines that loiter around even when I'm mad.

So as far as I'm concerned, this aging business has really gotten
old. But wait! New on the market is an oral spray we can get called

HGH (not to be confused with getting "HiGH"). Human Growth Hormone supposedly reverses old fogey symptoms with the added bonus of sprucing up one's love life.

Tempting, yes. But even if it made me ten years younger, I'd *still* have to behave like a responsible adult. And I'm expected to keep up the charade for the rest of my life—or at least 'til I enter my second childhood.

So now I can't wait to be a kid again.

HAVING A BAD HALO DAY

THANKS TO THE sins of a few and a whole lot of bad press, the number of Catholics has sharply declined. Though my faith didn't die, its life hung in the balance, and I confess I played hooky from church for a while.

But when I ran into our local priest at the post office one day, I took it as a sign. I leafed through my box of collection envelopes for the current date and hid the rejects in the recycle bin. Then I changed into my Sunday best and showed up for Mass. To my great relief, the roof remained intact.

This is not to say my attendance record is flawless. Our parish offers three services each weekend. If I don't make it to the first one, I set my sites on the other two. And if, on occasion, I miss them all, I blame it on any number of feeble excuses that sound perfectly valid at the time. They all boil down to one thing though: I'm having a bad halo day.

Since I'm 'fessing up here, I may as well admit I'm not a hundred percent attentive either. For some reason, my mind wanders during the Gospel readings no matter how hard I try to concentrate—and the mental hiatus kicks off shortly after the intro. Suddenly, a random thought pops into my head like, *Gee, did I shut off my car lights?* Soon it swells into a full-blown obsession that drives out all other notions, no matter how sacred.

But our pastor's sermons draw me back to the present. So much so, in fact, that I'd swear he writes each one for my ears only. Short and to the point, they focus on some issue I've wrestled with all week, as though he peeked in a window. Or listened with a chalice to the wall.

And they consistently inspire me to live a more noble life.

Temporarily anyway. I'm less likely, for instance, to count hypocrites *after* the homily than before. And I'm more tolerant of the singer behind me who, for the life of her, can't hit the proper note.

I know Mass is winding down when I hear a thundering herd of kneelers returned to their original position. And soon we're released to go out and practice our faith.

'Til we get it right.

THE NAME OF THE DAME

"PLEASE PASS THE potatoes, dear," said an acquaintance of mine to his bride of ten years.

"How sweet!" I gushed. "You still call her 'dear.'"

"That's because he forgot my name," quipped his wife. "And I call *him* 'dear' so I won't use one of my ex-husbands' names by mistake."

Sentimental or not, they have a point. Dealing with names can cause confusion. As someone with far too many aliases, I should know. But each one serves as a welcome substitute for my *real* handle. You've heard of name-droppers? Well, I'd like to drop mine. In a trash can.

Which is why I often refer to "Lois" in quotes. That way people think it's made up, like the identities in Dear Abby letters (i.e., "I'm writing about my brother-in-law, 'Bill'..."). Or else I follow it with an asterisk like they do in articles about crime victims. Has this ever happened to you? I spent ten-odd minutes reading what happened to Jane Doe the other day, only to learn that's not her real name.

One reason I don't like Lois* is because no one spells it right. It's *not* Louis or Louise, okay Mom? My spell checker even permits Louse, of all things.

Though I felt less critical of my maiden name, it, too, lacked pizzazz. Like many brides, I took my husband's name when we tied the knot. So what happened? He accused me of identity theft. For real. The last name didn't bother him so much as swiping his nickname for this column. So I withdrew it and for a while it was known as a farce with no name.

Frankly, I don't see what the big deal is. I'd be thrilled if someone stole *my* name. Then I could choose one with a little more class—like Geena Davis, for example.

In lieu of an identity change, I've assumed all manner of nicknames, especially in cyber space. Which one I use depends on who I e-mail. "Ois" derived when, as a child, I had trouble saying my L's, hence I sign messages to my dad as such. Thanks to typos, my sister knows me as "Oil" and my brother calls me "Loin."

But I answer to these handles as well as a swarm of other aliases. Because that's the name of the dame.

*Not her real name.

CONFESSIONS OF A CLOSET EATER

HEALTH-AND-FITNESS guru Jack LaLanne turns ninety this year. A *60 Minutes* interview revealed that he used to down a glass of blood each morning. Though he passes up plasma these days, he still hurls some curious cuisine into that juicer of his.

But I should talk. My eating habits are nothing to brag about either. As a young adult, I lived a Ho-Ho's throw from a sprawling supermarket. To satisfy a sweet tooth, I strolled over one day and purchased a can of frosting. Betty Crocker coconut-pecan, to be exact. Then I stole back to my apartment where I devoured every trace of it. We're talking a month's worth of sugar in one coma-inducing sitting.

I had suspected an eating disorder prior to that, but the frosting fiesta certainly drove home the point. Sweets weren't my sole downfall, however. I also bought into the chip theory that "no one can eat just one." Only I meant bag.

I would outweigh our upright if not for the fact I alternated these eating eras with health kicks. Like Jack LaLanne's, only less gory. At those times, I counted carbs, calories and the days 'til I could pig out again.

Despite twenty-six years of this nonsense, hope still springs eternal. Thus, I zealously cracked open a diet book called *Seven Secrets of Slim People* (Vikki Hansen and Shawn Goodman, authors).

Half of the "secrets" expand on what amounts to the Golden Rule—eat only when you are undeniably hungry. For yours truly, any number of emotions spark an impromptu feast. Boredom... frustration... anger...despair... But hunger? What a novel concept.

Another pointer involves eating consciously. *That's easy,* I thought. *I rarely dine in my sleep.* But in fact it means savoring each bite and focusing only on one's vittles. Never combine food with activities like reading, watching TV or—for the commuters among us—driving. I once ate entire meals on wheels.

My favorite tip in the book is to eat what we most desire. Don't munch on melba toast if you really crave sticky buns. The down side is that we're supposed to stop as soon as our hunger pangs cease. For most people, that means a mere fistful of food. Personally, I find it hard to quit when I'm on a roll. Or a can of frosting.

But it's worth a try.

NOT IN MY MAKEUP

SOME PEOPLE DREAM of being naked in public, but my chief nightmare involves baring my *face*. I harbor this fear of being seen without makeup. It may have a more technical term, but I call it cosmetophobia.

I'm not kidding. The house could be burning down to its last two-by-four and I'd be in the loo evening my brows. It goes without saying the first thing I'd save is my bag of tricks. Like VISA, it's everywhere I want to be.

The obsession started fresh out of high school when I received an invitation to a cosmetic party. It felt like I'd walked into the House of Mirrors, and I scoffed to myself at the primping guests. But soon, my "before" mug showed merciful improvement, and I humbly recruited.

Being a cosmetic queen ain't cheap. Even using bargain brands, I've washed off no less than five thousand dollars' worth of putty over the past three decades. Imagine the savings had I simply enlisted a few good paper bags. In case the first one broke.

Every bit as wasteful is the amount of time spent. Let's do the math here. Ten minutes a day times three hundred sixty-five days a year times twenty-eight years equals...carry the one...a total of seventeen *hundred* hours blown for the sake of vanity.

I've tried kicking the habit, but it's just not in my makeup. True, I've downsized a bit. I used to go to even greater lengths to ape those flawless dames in makeup ads. They're the picture of perfection—at least 'til I draw on facial hair.

These ads help sell an estimated twelve hundred tubes of lipstick per *minute*, according to the *Minnesota Daily Online*. But not to me. I gave that product the boot when I learned it contained urea. I asked myself, *Do I wanna brighten my kisser with something derived from pee? Maybe not.*

But I still use cosmetics to urge my peepers out of hiding. (If only eye pencils came with erasers.) And, chances are, I will 'til I cash in my chips.

I can just hear spectators at my funeral—those who show up out of curiosity.

"So *that's* what she looked like," they'll say.

Then the mortician will close the coffin, which, by prior arrangement, sports *two* lids. In case the first one breaks.

MURPHY'S LAW OF MOTOR MOUTHS

I HAD JUST READ about a celebrity who triumphed over cancer. Too bad it was an old article. Having heard nothing further, I mentioned the "survivor" in hopes of cheering a friend with the same disease.

"Look at Gilda Radner," I said with forced optimism.

The room grew far too quiet before my chum replied, "She's dead, Lois."

I call it Murphy's Law of Motor Mouths, and have blindly obeyed it most of my life. You name the occasion and, if I *can* say something wrong, I *do*. And I need the Jaws of Life™ to remove my foot.

This could be genetic, seeing as my sister recalls a similar moment. Her friend had recently lost a loved one and Joan did her best to keep the conversation light. So she rambled on about this great dish she tried at a new restaurant, which should have been a safe subject. But she followed it with, "Thought I died and went to heaven."

Where's Cyranno when you need him? You may recall the French character whose composition skills helped a less articulate friend win the hand (and other parts) of the fair Roxanne. Never mind he wanted her for himself. It occurs to me we could all use a personal coach like that now and then.

So I'm happy to tell you about a book out now called *Miss Manners' Basic Training: The Right Thing to Say* by Judith Martin. It covers not only solemn occasions, but blissful ones as well. You'd be surprised at the gems people come up with when a simple congratulations will do. For example:

Graduations—"But what does one do with a fine arts degree?"

Marriages—"Rotsa ruck!"

Births—"So *that's* why you got hitched."

Thanks to Miss Manners, we can all turn the perfect phrase in any situation without even having to think. In the interests of propriety, though, we should consult the manual ahead of time. It might look a bit odd flipping wildly through its pages before speaking. And rehearsing ain't a bad idea either.

Neither precursor is necessary when writing, of course, be it kudos or notes of sympathy. But my concern in either case involves sincerity. How heartfelt can it be if someone else thought up your dialogue ahead of time?

Still, it beats the boners I've uttered over the years. As a Murphy's Law-abiding citizen.

JUST SAY THE "N" WORD

PUNY THOUGH IT is, I tend to wrestle with the word "no." And nine times out of ten, I get pinned.

When someone asks me to do this or that, I inevitably assume the obligation, no matter how crammed my Day-Timer may be. With a reputation like that, I receive more requests than the Average Jo Ann. An acquaintance will call with still another favor and I hear myself say, "Sure, I'll jump off the Mackinac Bridge—no problem. What's that? I need to find a sponsor?"

Thus goes the life (and death) of a hopeless people pleaser. Not a healthy situation. Even without the plunge, my wellness is directly related to my ability, or inability, to say no. Other areas may be gravely affected, too—like the time I made a few hundred programs for a nonprofit group and fried my beloved copier.

From whence does this blind obedience come? A deep-seated fear of not being liked? Or is it to ward off the guilt that stems from saying no? And is that a girl thing? Very few men seem familiar with that emotion. I know guys behind *bars* who don't feel guilty.

But I digress. The issue, as I recall, is my trouble with the "N" word. But I'm taking great pains to change, and have found a number of ways to do this. One method requires no speaking at all. I simply go about my business wearing a sandwich sign labeled "No Dumping."

For requests that prompt a verbal reply, I can voice what a former co-worker used to say. "Sorry, that's not in my job description."

Or I can express it in any number of languages. A web site I stumbled over (www.elite.net/~runner/jennifers/no.htm) lists five hundred-twenty foreign words that mean the same thing.

In Navajo one would say "dooda," which sounds far less lethal. The word for "no" in Northern Ghana is "aye," so voting must be a real hoot there. My favorite, though, would have to be Tatar-speaking Russians who just say "yuk."

Another site (www.mentalsoup.com/mentalsoup/101ways.htm) offers a hundred and one offbeat ways to say no. For example, "I have to study for a blood test."

Using the above techniques, I'm making gradual progress. And some day I'll find it a cinch to say no. And not just to my Better Half.

BE NOT A CHICKEN

ROBERT FROST ONCE said, "There's nothing I'm afraid of like scared people." Good thing he never met me. Despite being acrophobic, I take cowardice to new heights.

That was, in fact, the first fear I acquired, though its name escaped me. I was all of six at the time, and debating whether or not to jump off the porch. Alas, I chickened out. And as I grew, so did my list of anxieties.

"I have more fears than Freud had patients," I told my family the other day. Then I rattled off a dozen.

"Don't forget atmosphere," my son, Kelly, quipped.

"What kind of phobia is that?" I asked.

"The fear of air."

But I'm not the Lone Ranger. It appears everyone is afraid of *something*, as witnessed by Phobialist.com, a worldwide roster of fears.

Some folks have geliophobia, the fear of laughter. As a humor columnist, I fear people who fear laughter. Fortunately (for me, at least) I don't have verbophobia, the fear of words. Nor do I suffer from amathophobia, the fear of dust, as anyone could tell from my housekeeping.

I don't have proctophobia either, which is the fear of rectums. Another anxiety involving body parts is geniophobia, the fear of chins. And people with more than one chin probably suffer from catoptrophobia, the fear of mirrors.

The mother of all fears is phobophobia, the fear of phobias. We have nothing to fear but fear of fears itself.

Thankfully, there are several ways to conquer our anxieties. One method is called desensitization. This involves training the scared-out-of-his-wits patient to respond to fear with relaxation. In my case, that would be easier said than done.

Another procedure used is exposure treatment. That technique requires us phobics to be exposed to the stimulus we fear until the emotion fades away.

This, so I'm told, is the basis for the controversial show, *Fear Factor*. A recent episode saw players removing smashed insects from a car window with their mouths. I find it hard to swallow that each of them feared this situation before producers dreamed it up. If so, their therapy sessions probably went like this:

Patient: "So what d'ya think, Doc?"

Doctor: "I think you suffer from clean-your-windshield-orally-phobia."

On the other hand, to be a contestant on the show, I would have to wear a bikini on national TV.

Now *that's* a scary thought.

PLAYING TAG SALE

IT TOOK FAR more time to set up than I planned. And as I toiled, more than one passerby asked the silly question, "Are you having a tag sale?"

"Yeah," I wanted to say, "and you're it." Either that or, "No, I'm just airing out my wardrobe." But I stifled the urge and answered politely.

My Better Half being none too keen on these ventures, I performed my own labor. In all, I made a few hundred trips to the basement. By the time I wrestled a mattress up the stairs, I felt a deep need to pass out on it.

Normally bargain hunters arrive at the very start of a sale, if not two hours early. So I sensed a problem when no one showed up right away. A little voice inside me gibed, *It's nine o'clock. Do you know where your customers are?*

It couldn't have been the weather, which was sunny and warm—unlike my disposition. *Maybe it's my inventory?* I wondered. But, no, I had all the usual merchandise. Clothing of all sizes... A library's worth of books... Virgin exercise equipment...

I also offered items not normally found at your average sale. Like, who else in town would sell feminine hygiene products? (Don't laugh—someone bought 'em.) There was even a dressmaker's dummy on which I hung a coat. I left it unbuttoned to expose the mannequin, which looked, for all the world, like an exhibitionist. But, perverted or not, at least it kept me company.

Still, there was ample time to ponder my lack of customers. Yeah, I'd placed an ad in the paper. Yeah, I'd put up signs around town. Hmmm...maybe it's my mouthwash...

Oh, a few people came by each hour, but most of them left with their wallets intact. Perhaps they were put off by the lack of price tags.

"Make an offer!" I'd cried out when they looked vaguely interested.

"Okay," one guy replied. "Nothing."

At one point, four potential patrons appeared out of nowhere and I raced to get my camera. But they left before I could record the uncommon event.

"You're not very busy," a lady observed a while later, stating the obvious.

"You missed the rush," I grumbled.

Eventually time ran out like my customers and I bundled my belongings and hauled them away. And next time I play tag sale, it'll be in someone else's yard.

WHERE THE SUN DOESN'T SHINE

"WHY DON'T YOU get some sun?" taunted a former boss with a year-round tan. As a hopeless whitey, I took offense to that remark. I also took a trip to the store for tanning lotion. Back then there wasn't the variety you see today. As I recall, I found one lone brand which came in three no-brainer shades: Light, medium and Guess-Who's-Coming-to-Dinner.

Now there are dozens to choose from, each offering varying degrees of SPF (Shedding Pale Face). I read about a Swedish tanning lotion out now that contains caviar. That explains its champagne price, but why would people knowingly coat their body with fish eggs? And what if they meet a romantic roughy at the beach?

But I should talk. I used a formula last year that should have stayed on the shelf. Cracking it open released the odor of something our beagle would have happily rolled in.

You don't need sun to get a tan these days as loads of lotions will tint you in the privacy of your own home. You must spread it on evenly, however, to prevent that "bar code" look. And avoid sitting unless you want to give your new mauve sofa mahogany stripes.

Some people prefer using a tanning bed. This looks like a brightly lit coffin and enjoys a similar price range. It comes with a timer so you don't need a toothpick inserted to know you're done.

Another option in the bathing beauty department is the tan-through swimsuit. This allows us to brown every square inch of ourselves without facing arrest. The special fabric acts as a screen, so one need not apply lotion where the sun doesn't normally shine.

According to the ad, their big selling point is that you can tan "without any unsightly lines at the neck and arms." It seems to me that "unsightly" is in the eye of the beholder. Personally, I like having *proof* I'm getting brown—like the puppy that pulls on the toddler's shorts in that tanning lotion ad. When people doubt my progress, I can nudge my watchband aside for irrefutable evidence.

Unless I moon them.

THE GRATING OUTDOORS

I LIVE MERE BLOCKS from the Bay de Noc shoreline. To fishermen and swimming enthusiasts, it is nothing short of heaven. But the day I spent at the beach last week was no day at the beach.

Being allergic to water, I settled my middle-aged bod on a towel while my son and Better Half frolicked in the waves. Tugging discreetly to keep my suit in place, I looked around to see if anyone noticed. Luckily, my fellow beachgoers were too busy flirting. I found them far more fascinating than they found me.

Eventually I turned my attention to a book I'd brought and fought a typhoon over when to turn the pages. Despite that and the sand that blew in my eyes, I became quite engrossed and lost all track of time.

The result, as any moron could guess, was a dandy case of sunburn. As you may know, skin continues burning for twelve hours after you've packed up your picnic. By the time it quit, the "little bit of color" I'd sought turned out to be scarlet. One could almost smell the odor of searing flesh.

Darn close to needing skin grafting, I pulled on civilian clothes with all the limberness of the Tin Man. The act of sitting brought unbridled discomfort. Not a fan of pain, I spent as much time as possible in a vertical position.

This strategy made sleep difficult, however, and in the wee hours of the morning, I finally gave in. Cautiously, I slid myself between the sheets, which felt as smooth as burlap.

Showering the next day had its difficulties, too. It proved to be ethnic water torture with a new wrinkle. Speaking of new wrinkles, well...never mind. At any rate, I let myself "air dry" like dishes rather than towel off what remained of my skin.

After a few days of this nonsense, a lingering itch developed—the kind that even bear claws can't satisfy. Scratching myself as nonchalantly as possible, I vowed to never again get burned.

According to the Center for Disease Control and Prevention, I could have saved myself worlds of grief by taking any of the following suggestions:

(a) Stay in the shade.

(b) Wear protective clothing.

(c) Use a wide-brimmed hat.

(d) Rub on sunscreen.

To play it safe, I plan to implement all four. Next time I visit the grating outdoors.

FIRST THING IN THE MOURNING

EVERY TOWN HAS a resident funeral crasher. Whether he knows the deceased or not, he shows up to cash in on the free lunch that follows. I find this ironic since I'd sooner go bald than attend a service.

I don't share grief well and prefer to be alone first thing in the mourning. This is because I am a crier and a noisy one at that. Even when I keep boo-hoos and assorted hiccups to a respectable volume, my subsequent sniffs give me away.

A friend of mine, who is also prone to tears, said she has a personal strategy for occasions like that: Don't *look* at anything sad. (The photo collage, for example.) Don't *listen* to anything sad. (Music invariably does me in.) And don't *touch* anything sad. (Nothing opens the flood gates like a hug.) But they won't let me in wearing blinders, earplugs, and a straitjacket.

And the older I get, the more funerals I have to attend. With all that practice, you'd think I'd have bereavement down pat by now. But I get so worked up, I'm lucky if I remember a hanky.

So I was grateful to find a box of Kleenex in every pew at a recent church service. Each one glided back and forth along its designated route like a printer cartridge. Since criers outnumbered non-criers in my row, our allotment ran out quickly, and I had to wrestle a lady for the last one.

The seasoned mourner plans ahead for a tissue shortage. She tucks a hanky for tears in one pocket and one for nose blowing in the other. And she makes a supreme effort to remember which is which.

I wish I'd done that for another funeral I attended. When I reached in my pocket I found nothing but lint which—trust me—makes a sorry substitute. In the end, I was forced to use someone's *pre-owned* tissue. I'd expand on that, but I assume you get the picture.

If I could just detach myself from the situation a bit, I wouldn't *need* tissue. So I'm pushing for a drive-thru funeral home like they have in big cities. One can pay her respects, make a donation, and even choose a floral arrangement from the safety of her own car.

They could call it Life in the Taps Lane.

ACCI-DENTS HAPPEN

THE FIRST ONE wasn't my fault. An elderly guy ran a yield sign and our cars mated in the intersection. I stepped out timidly to assess the damage and frowned at the dent in my bumper.

"No need to report this," the man said. "There's barely a scratch."

A rookie driver, I naively thought he had my best interests in mind and bid him adieu. Then it dawned on me I'd have to pay the fender bender mender myself.

Acci-dent number two occurred the same year on an unfamiliar street in an equally unfamiliar town. A bit of advice here: one should only drive one way on a one-way street, and that way is *with* traffic. Or risk a one-way ticket to the slammer.

The third hit came a decade later when I stopped for a red light, but the car behind me kept going. "Who's the numbskull...?" I muttered to myself. But the driver was none other than a dear friend I hadn't seen in years. We hugged and reminisced, holding up traffic and baffling witnesses at the scene.

My fourth and last collision (to date) was not as bittersweet. I honestly thought the light would stay yellow, but the son-of-a-gun turned red. And since the crash attracted cop cars, a wrecker and tons of unwanted attention, *I* turned red as well. As luck would have it, I had just filled the gas tank. And if all *that* weren't bad enough, the impact caused my normally loyal bladder to betray me, laying to rest the clean-underwear theory.

This last crash induced a tangible fear of driving, and though I've gotten back on the hoss when necessary, it is with great reluctance. Suffice it to say, I maintain a safe distance between other cars and mine—that being roughly a train-length.

As a result of this cautious mentality, I make a rather jumpy passenger. Ask anyone who chauffeurs me. When I perceive a hairy situation, my right foot springs up of its own accord and stomps on an invisible brake, which drives drivers to distraction.

"Down, girl!" I hiss at the lively limb.

But at least it means well. Not like that Texas woman who mowed down her cheating husband with a Mercedes. She claimed it was an accident, but the jury found otherwise.

That must make it an on-purpose-dent.

VOICING A MEDICAL COMPLAINT

BE CAREFUL WHAT you wish for, the saying goes. I used to wish I could ditch my Mickey Mouse voice but now, thanks to a viral infection, I can impersonate Kermit the Frog.

It all started a few weeks ago when I swallowed a set of Ginsu knives—or at least that's how my throat felt. Soon after, I lost my voice, much to my husband's delight. A few days later, the virus spread to my peepers, turning them a vivid shade of red.

The ailment showed no signs of departing, so I called for a doctor's appointment and described my symptoms. The receptionist found my name in her computer fairly quickly. "Here you are," she said. "You were born in 1922?"

"Er—no," I croaked. "I may *sound* eighty-two, but I'm only forty-something."

"Oh," she said. "In that case, the doctor can't see you unless you're a regular patient."

"How can I be a regular patient if he won't see me?" I whispered hoarsely.

So she asked me some standard new-patient questions that my

voice box strained to answer.

"And do you have any health problems?" she went on.

"You're kidding, right?"

Before long I found myself in a waiting room with another patient suffering from pink eye. We looked like twin rabbits. Soon I was whisked into an exam room where my vitals were checked.

A strong, silent type, the resident on duty uttered few words before embarking on his mission. Armed with an otoscope he examined nearly every orifice I own. What bothered me was the order in which they were checked. Call me picky, but I prefer he'd thrust that instrument in my mouth *before* it probed my nose and ears.

Moments later he scrawled out a set of prescriptions and I went on my mired way. But despite the official doctor visit and taking an assortment of meds, I'm still dragging my derriere. And I embarrass myself periodically by breaking into coughing fits without notice.

It happened again on the phone the other day. A word caught in my throat and, before long, I was inches away from swallowing my tongue.

So I'm anxious to recover my good health. And if my normally piercing Mickey-Mouse voice ever returns, I'll never again wish for a new one.

THE BREATH OF DEATH

YOU MAY RECALL the dental employee I riled, who wrote a scathing letter to the editor. She said I was the type to "call the dentist at home, two a.m., on any given holiday...expecting to be seen because of...a broken tooth." As it turned out, she was psychic.

Well, sort of. I didn't call him at home and it wasn't two a.m. but, yes indeed, I broke a tooth. And I made the appointment on none other than National Goof Off Day.

Fact is, the tooth cracked a few weeks before that. I first noticed it when my tongue took inventory and came up short. At that point I should have phoned my dentist for the preventive dentistry the psychic employee mentioned in her letter. But instead, I ignored the problem in hopes it would go away.

Then one day I noticed a truly revolting taste in my mouth. The mere description would induce vomiting, so I'll keep the particulars to myself. But suffice it to say, it had a dire effect on my breath.

"You need to eat something," my husband, Dan, announced.

"I just did," I replied.

"I hate to say this but your breath is making me sick."

"How do you think *I* feel?"

I was curious as to the cause, but too chicken to look. As luck would have it, the development occurred on a weekend, so Dr. Dan filled in and dispensed some unsolicited advice.

"Rinse with hydrogen peroxide after every meal," he instructed me.

I wrinkled my nose. "Isn't that used in hair color?"

As Chief of the Dental Police, he then placed me under surveillance. "I haven't seen you rinse and spit yet," he stated late in the day.

"Like I'm gonna do that with an audience."

At eight o'clock the next morning, give or take a nanosecond, I called my friendly neighborhood dentist.

"What seems to be the problem?" asked the receptionist.

"I have swollen gums, a missing tooth and my breath could sink tall ships."

Thanks to her, I got in right away. The patients in the waiting room kept their distance, and my fumes assaulted the dentist as well. But with a minimum of fanfare, he dislodged the infected tooth and banished forever the breath of death. At least 'til the next emergency.

I should phone that psychic employee to find out what it'll be.

ALL IN A DAY'S WALK

AFTER AN EXTENDED leave of absence, I'm back to my favorite form of exercise. I like walking because it requires no coordination. At least *most* of the time. I tripped on uneven pavement the other day and glanced around red-faced to see who'd noticed. Luckily no one had, so I got up and continued on.

Thanks to some helpful gear, I trek two miles each morning regardless of conditions. True, sunglasses look a little odd in cloudy weather, but they serve as a windshield, halting errant bugs in mid-flight. Too bad my shades don't come with wiper blades.

Likewise, my ever-present umbrella raises eyebrows on a sunny day. "Is it supposed to rain?" a neighbor asked a while back, looking confused.

"Nope," I said. "This is my shillelagh." Because not only does it shield me from showers and the occasional sprinkler, it's also a ready form of self-defense. Like a Swiss army knife, it has other functions, too. I use it for a trash picker-upper when necessary as well as a baton to lead the band in my head...

...because, of course, I'm wired for sound, thanks to a gift from my Better Half. It took a while to get used to my new cassette player though. "These headphones keep sliding off my ears," I griped after returning with them wrapped around my neck.

"You're wearing them upside down," Dan explained, shaking his head over my mental deficiency.

"Hey!" I replied. "Nowhere in this multi-language instruction manual does it tell how to put them on."

According to the self-improvement tapes I listen to, I used even *less* than two percent of my brain's capacity. Now that I'm in the know, the Walkman has become a constant companion on my daily journeys. But whether I hear motivational tapes or golden oldies, I've discovered one drawback: its ceaseless appetite for batteries. I know it's time to change them when the Bee Gees sing bass.

And regardless of what's playing, it's hard to hear folks I meet along the way. When they call out a friendly greeting, I just smile and nod, with no earthly idea of what was said. For all I know, it could be, "Your barn door is open."

But as they say, it's all in a day's walk.

SCRAPBOOKING WITHOUT A GLUE GUN

I LAUNCHED A NEW hobby this year. That means one more thing vying for that spare time I'm rumored to have.

But scrapbooking is the perfect pastime for shutterbugs, and it requires little investment. According to idea magazines on the market, one need only buy tape or glue and an assortment of stencils, stickers, die cuts, rubber stamps, paper punches and decorative scissors. Not to mention an empty forty-dollar scrapbook.

Oops! You'll need paper, too. Supply companies warn us to use only the acid-free variety, which means it doesn't take drugs.

Of all the above-named provisions, my favorite is stickers. Thanks to my cousin, Candy, I have enough stickers to last 'til I'm stiff, but now I'm addicted to them. As luck would have it, my ten-year-old lost interest in them a few years back. But I've coached him to just say yes when businesses offer him one. It's the least he can do for his mother.

Materials aren't cheap, so I submit sales slips to my insurance company. After all, it's good therapy. So much so that if my house burned down, the first thing I'd grab is my scrapbook supplies. I corral them in a nice portable container that outweighs me by several pounds.

Unlike regular photo albums, scrapbooks incorporate themes. Instead of just one dorky picture, they feature a whole collage. Consequently, I hold my subjects hostage 'til I have enough for a two-page spread.

Cropping makes use of those iffy shots, but I tend to go overboard lopping off the bad parts. This carries over into other areas as well. The other day I cropped my son's toast and it wound up the size of a postage stamp.

While veteran scrapbookers create virtual works of art, I'm still in the novice stage. Furthermore, too much adhesive made some of my pages stick together. But I switched to tape so now I'm scrapbooking without a glue gun.

Though I'm still on my first album, I have big plans for future books. Among other topics, they will spotlight former employers and exciting events like the time we repaired our sidewalk.

"Why would you want to remember those things?" asked my husband, Dan, with a laugh.

"Suppose I lose my memory some day," I replied. "Looking through these albums may help bring it back."

This prompted him to give me the look. "Or make you glad you forgot."

MURDER, SHE READ

I'VE BEEN ON a murder kick lately. No, I haven't snuffed anyone's life out—though there's been ample cause at times. What I mean is, I'm fascinated with true crime stories. Luckily, stores stock a never-ending supply of these, thanks to man- and womankind's inability to get along.

This new passion is not necessarily a good development. For one thing, homicide makes a poor choice for bedtime reading on the off chance one plans to sleep afterward. Dozing is unlikely when my heart threatens to squeeze out my throat and run for cover.

Moreover, I'm reluctant to turn out the lights when drowsiness finally occurs. And only the most urgent nature calls succeed in luring me downstairs where potential killers lurk. I know they're there from faint noises they make. It's mere coincidence they show up only on nights I read murder tales.

Furthermore, it takes forever to get through these books. My current choice bursts with five hundred pages of fine print. Way beyond describing the murder, it sets forth life stories of the victim, the killer, the investigator, and every Tom, Dick and Harriet they meet.

Still, it's hard to put down and I sneak in a few passages every chance I get. When suspense gets too high and a stroke seems imminent, I peek at the ending to find out how the killer gave him- (or her-) self away and stealthily work my way back.

This current killer craze promotes rampant paranoia, too. The assassins all seem like your Average Joe (or Josephine) before their crimes come to light. Consequently, I find myself suspecting everyone I meet of foul play. The pizza guy...the Avon Lady...the Boy Scout adopting an elm... Why, even the *tree* isn't above suspicion.

The only person I haven't suspected is my son, Kelly, who would least benefit from my demise. I could learn a lesson from him. He focuses on more lighthearted reading before turning out his light. I found evidence of this while making his bed one morning, when a computer manual and five joke books were tangled in the sheets.

On the plus side, reading true crime stories burns more calories than tearing through, say, *Webster's Dictionary*. The resulting pulse rate rivals the toughest workouts, and it sure beats running laps. To say nothing of aerobics.

Now *those* are murder.

YOU SLEEP, YOU REAP

I ENVY MY COMPUTER. It has this sleep button you can press that instantly prompts a siesta. People press my buttons all day long and I *still* can't doze at night.

There are a number of reasons for this. Often it's because I go over prior events or conversations in my mind. Whether they occurred the day before or the previous decade, they replay themselves like a VCR on auto pilot.

Another nocturnal habit I engage in is obsession over real or imagined medical problems. I have, for example, this growth on my head the size of a robin's egg. It's been there fore years and I rarely think about it. But sometimes at night, it creeps into my thoughts and I fret over, among other things, its chances of hatching.

Vanity also plays a part in insomnia. On those rare occasions I have a good hair day, I try to lay "just so" on my pillow to keep from messing up my 'do. Or I'll train myself to turn over now and then to squash each side symmetrically. So much for beauty rest.

This is ironic, considering the effects of a sleepless night. I used to have little circles under my eyes. Now they're hula hoops. Forget the saying, "You snooze, you lose." Truth is, "You sleep, you reap." But I haven't had much of a harvest lately.

There's no one to blame but myself though. Like the Ricardos, my Better Half and I discovered the joy of separate bunks. That way my hot flashes don't roast him, and he can snore all he wants without a jab in the ribs.

This also gives me room to stretch out on my back, flop on my stomach, or curl into a tight little ball. Okay, a big ball.

But even as a slumber party of one, sleep eludes me. And the more I focus on it, the less I can do it. Consequently, I lay awake 'til all hours reading. Last night I scanned one of those women's magazines that run self-help articles. This one asked the question, "Do you have a sleeping disorder?"

"*Hrmph.*" I snorted. "Does a shrink have a couch?"

Chronic insomniacs, it said, should see a doctor. So I made an appointment for me and my 'puter. For a sleep button transplant.

IN HOT PURSE-UIT

TO HEAR HIM tell it, our first date saw me in a state of high anxiety. As we rode down the street, says Dan, I clung to my purse like a vinyl security blanket. My future husband tried to oust it to the back seat, but I refused to surrender it.

What he didn't realize is that I've always been possessive about my handbag. Or maybe I should say handbags, seeing as a number of them vie for my attention. But whichever one I choose, we're as tight as a tube top.

You've heard of clutch purses? Well, I take mine literally. In fact, I hold it in more of a death grip. So I prefer the shoulder strap variety, though at times it wraps around me like a python. Less confining, but every bit as safe, is the fanny pack, which frees my arms with the added bonus of hiding my gut.

Why this need for security? Because, humble though it is, I prefer my home sweet home to any place else on earth. When I leave, my only link to it is the creature comforts lurking in my purse. Consequently, I cram as much in there as humanly possible.

That can mean any number of personal items which, being personal, I won't mention. I also toss in a couple of time-passers, should I find myself bored. These include, among other things, a deck of cards and the latest gotta-read-it paperback. And as a wannabe writer, I tote along a pad, pen and ten-thousand-word dictionary. All things considered, I would have made a swell carpetbagger.

You'd think with an inventory like that, I'd have provisions for any occasion, but au contraire. I needed emergency Kleenex the other day, but came up short. Even the paper wad crammed in new purses would have helped.

Therein lies the biggest drawback to having more than one handbag. Like the Changing of the Guards, I methodically transfer necessities from one to another, but they don't always fit. Furthermore, I find that the cuter the purse, the less functional it is. I'm lucky if it can hold my house key and still close.

So I'm in hot purse-uit of a more practical handbag—something big enough to corral my cargo. And when filled to capacity, could anchor the Titanic.

GIVE ME FIVE (HUNDRED)

BELIEVE IT OR not, you're reading my five-hundredth column—unless you stop here and skip to the comics. But since this is Be Kind to Editors and *Writers* Month, the least you can do is finish it.

For the most part, the feedback generated by "Jest for Fun" has warmed my heart and inflated my hat size. But I've received plenty of thumps on the head over the years, too. Like the lady who bristled over my brassiere article. If it were graded, she'd give it a triple D.

I still ponder over a comment I received from a local celebrity. "You're...evolving," she said, groping for the right word.

"Into what?" I wanted to ask.

As a whole, men are more complimentary. I'll never forget the fellow who gushed, "I see your column in the paper all the time! I use it to wrap fish."

But they are just as likely to inform me when I err. Like a column I wrote about sports that declared, "You never hear of a team called the Gophers." Roughly five thousand Gopher fans were quick to correct me on that issue.

Though I proofread each week's offering a few dozen times, I miss typos on occasion. Unfortunately, they are not missed by readers. Luckily, there are still some folks who hold the dubious belief I know what I'm doing.

I'll never forget the time my husband was late getting home from work and a cop car pulled up to the curb. With a heavy heart, I prepared myself for the worst. But the guy in blue merely asked me to edit a story he'd written.

Speaking of my hubby, a few readers have remarked that my articles take jabs at him. And I recently received a scathing but anonymous note from some dame who said Dan should "ditch" me. This amused my Better Half, who gives his blessing to all feud columns before they go to press. And I'd like to take this time to thank him for—er—providing so much material.

I've gotten a big bang out of my fifteen minutes of microscopic fame. Every so often a total stranger will ask if I'm "the writer." Depending on how bad that week's column is, I may or not admit it.

But since it's Be Kind to Editors and *Writers* Month, I think I'll 'fess up 'til it's over.

IGNORANCE IS BLISSIUM

I HEARD ABOUT IT on the radio one day and called the 800-number. "You've reached the Blissium Hot Line and my name's Steve," said a smooth voice. "How are you today?"

"Kinda down," I replied. "I had a fight with my husband this morning. Then I got a rejection in the mail and—" Normally I don't spill my guts to a stranger like that, but since he sold an anti-depressant, I thought he should know. "—so I'm calling to find out about Blissium," I said, after spewing forth my reasons for the blues.

Happy to have one on the line, Steve told me about the relatively new product—or rather, what it *isn't*. "Blissium is *not* a drug," he stressed. "It's *not* habit forming and will *not* produce a hangover."

"Yes, but what *is* it?" I asked.

"It's an herbal supplement that makes people feel...euphoric."

"Herbs?" asked I, recalling the diet aid that gave me hives. "What kind of herbs?"

He rattled off a dozen ingredients. "Passion flower, hops, catnip and folate. Folate is an impor—"

"Catnip?" I interrupted. "There's catnip in it??"

"It's been found to be an effective mood elevator."

"Beats taking the stairs." I snorted, and whooped it up over the joke. "But, seriously," I said after regaining control. "How can you tell it improves one's frame of mind? My cat never smiles."

From his deep intake of breath, I sensed that Steve wasn't as blissful as he'd been earlier, so I changed the subject. "How soon does this stuff take effect?"

Steve cleared his throat. "Blissium works in fifteen minutes. The daytime formula lasts a full eight hours. You also get the after dark formula to take just before bedtime."

"Why would I do that?" I asked. "When I'm unconscious, I don't care if I'm happy or not."

"Some...people...can't *sleep*...when they're...depressed!" he said, obviously through clenched teeth.

"I s'pose not," I agreed. "So...how do I get my free sample?"

"We don't *give* free samples. But we do offer a money-back guarantee if you're not absolutely delighted."

"Delightful. How much loot are we talking about?"

"For only seventy-five-ninety-five, you receive a full one-month supply."

"What would it cost for a few hours of elation?" I quipped.

"We don't sell in smaller quantities!" Steve bellowed.

"Geez, what a grouch!" I said. "Just one more question...why don't *you* take it?"

THA...THA...THAT'S ALL, FOLKS! (OR NOT)

I POPPED A BUSHEL of popcorn and snuggled in to watch a video the other night. But anticipation rapidly turned to disappointment. I'd rented a sequel, forgetting that successor movies are rarely success*ful*. You know how credits appear at the end of a show? Well, this one listed *dis*credits.

I can count on Edward's Scissorhand the number of sequels as good as their predecessors. The mistake producers make is that they must go to great lengths to outdo the original. More special effects, more nudity, more blood and guts—we're literally talking overkill here. All of this excess, of course, is designed to make them more moolah. But it only makes viewers morose.

If you saw *Rambo* and its umpteen sequels, you know what I mean. Each show saw him progressively more heroic. By the last flick, he could part the Red Sea with his right hand while performing heart surgery with his left. On himself.

Have movie makers never heard of the term "less is more?" Do we really need to see twelve cars blow up when a mere Yugo will suffice? Or watch more unsuspecting swimmers get chewed up and spit out? And how *could* they be unsuspecting if they saw the first *Jaws* flick?

For the most part, movie sequels are Number Two in more ways than one. And producers don't quit with that digit—often there's a third, fourth, and even fifth. What *is* this—a miniseries? Enough already!

Having belabored my point and then some, I admit a few sequels actually turn out as well as their predecessors. Though I haven't personally seen these, general consensus includes *Indiana Jones, Star Wars* and anything starring California's new governor.

So I'm not completely against the concept. But producers should stick with shows that inspire a natural consequence. Sometimes, in fact, certain movies scream for a sequel. I'd like to see these titles make it to the screen:

404 Dalmatian Puppies
A Star Retires
The Birds II: At the Car Wash
Butch Cassidy and the Sundance Geezer
Conan the Rebuilder
Driving Miss Daisy's Hearse
Fiddler on the Ground: Force of Gravity
Guess Who's Washing the Dishes?
And last but not least:
Karate Codger

Maybe some day these will make it to celluloid (not to be confused with cellulite). 'Til then I'll snuggle in with a good book instead.

CHAPTER 4 – ALL IN THE GAME SHOW

GETTING REAL(ITY)

ACCORDING TO A RECENT poll, only two people on the planet have never watched *Survivor* and they both live in this house.

In case you've forgotten, each series introduces sixteen contestants—eight of each sex—with a wide variety of ethnic backgrounds. Each one tests his or her mettle (and greed) against the other fifteen in hopes of winning a million clams. If you do the math, you know that each has a six-and-a-quarter percent chance, which beats Lotto all to heck.

The contest takes place in selected remote locales that just happen to have the resources for a TV production crew. This is good news for rabid viewers. Why? Though they may have had a general idea where Africa was, how many could have found Pulau Tiga on a map before? Better question: how many had even *heard* of Pulau Tiga? So, from an educational standpoint, the series gets a big thumbs up. Sort of a Reality Geography Bee with some drama thrown in.

Now add to that formula a little discomfort. In their efforts to survive, contestants must sometimes do unpleasant things, like devouring grub worms. To that I say, big deal! I know a guy who eats nightcrawlers for free.

A tougher challenge is when they are asked questions and have to write the answers down on paper. This has happened to me at baby showers, and I can assure you it's no picnic.

Those who can't pass muster are voted off the island by their fellow castaways. These deportments always make big news. The resulting media coverage is right up there with terrorist attacks.

C'mon, guys—it's not like they *died* or anything. Chances are, they'll use their newly acquired fame to hit the talk show circuit. They'll ride the crest by signing autographs and handing out eight-by-ten glossies. And then they'll go on to star in movies, after which they'll run for president.

This is not reality, people! If the producer wants a *real* reality show, he should film these individuals in a typical American job. Over the course of the series, they must try to juggle day care, home obligations, and the nine-to-five grind without going Looney Tunes. And if no one loses it and blows away his fellow co-workers, they *all* share the million bucks.

I wonder if they'd get any takers.

IT'S ALL IN THE GAME SHOW

AS A CONFIRMED OVER-REACTER, I'd make a dandy game show contestant. Ever watch those programs? With all the screaming and carrying on they do, you'd think *The Price is Right* was a horror picture. And a grown woman made a fool of herself doing cartwheels in front of a *Wheel of Fortune* audience. So, in other words, I'd fit right in.

Of course, it depends on the game, too. Hopefuls on *Jeopardy* are quite a bit more subdued than those on other shows. The exciting clamor of the Daily Double brings little more than a stifled yawn. Just once I'd like to see those intellectual types cut loose and let 'er rip—possibly going so far as to smile.

I'm not good at subdued, having been born a melodramatic type person. As an infant, I wore my heart on my diaper. Childhood allowed a full range of emotions as well—at least until reaching my teens. At that point I learned that it's not the least bit cool to get excited over things.

In an effort to fit in, I squelched my enthusiasm when it threatened to make an appearance, but it was with deep reluctance on my part. To thine own self be blue.

But underneath it all, I felt more like that famous rock-and-roll fan who was interviewed about her favorite group. It was the mid-Sixties, Beetle-mania was at an all-time peak, and she shrieked, cried and generally gave way to hysterics. Radio stations still play the audio, much to the fifty-some-year-old's embarrassment.

Now that I've grown up (more or less), I've freed my feelings and made up for lost time. They showed themselves during a nail-biting football game I watched a while back. It was fourth down and my team trailed as the final seconds ticked by. The Packers were a few yards from the goal and I was a few inches from a seizure. And when they scored, I lost it completely.

A guy in the room looked at me as though I should lease a padded cell. "I don't see what the big deal is," he said blandly.

His reaction was as foreign to me as mine was to him. Come to think of it, he'd make a great *Jeopardy* contestant.

I'll take Sour Pusses for Ten, Alex.

A LITTLE PHIL DIRT

I MAY SEEM LIKE a well-adjusted columnist but, truth is, I see a shrink on a regular basis. As is customary, each session finds me reclined on the couch in a comfortable position as I pour out a personal problem. I thought therapists were supposed to be good listeners but, in fact, Dr. Phil does most of the talking.

Then again, who am I to look gift therapy in the mouth? Thanks to the *Oprah* spin-off, I can draw professional advice for everything from weight woes to anger management. And it doesn't cost an arm and a ligament.

For those not in the know, here's the dirt on Phil: After earning his psychology degree, Phillip McGraw started your basic, run-of-the-mind therapy practice. When he realized it wasn't his "thing," he launched Courtroom Sciences, Inc., which helped Oprah in her defense against the cattlemen. Hence the connection.

I'm amazed at how many people volunteer to be analyzed. After they unload, Dr. Phil often bawls them out and nine out of ten dissolve into tears. Furthermore, most of his patients are women. Does that mean we ladies have more hang-ups? Or that we're more likely to seek help in front of a national TV audience?

Tuning in has its drawbacks though—most notably, the power of suggestion. Like everyone else, I have certain established anxieties. But then an episode will air beyond that realm and I think, *Yeah, I've felt like that at times.* And soon I'm adding *another* neurosis to my belt.

I wondered what kind of doctor Dr. Phil is. A psychiatrist? A podiatrist? Or some other -iatrist? So I checked out his web site (www.drphil.com) and learned he's a psychologist. So, by the way, is his son, Jay, who appears with him on the show occasionally. Clearly an underachiever, twenty-five-year-old Jay is also a licensed pilot, has a black belt, and published two books that lounged on the *New York Times* bestseller list.

Psychologists often draw from a professional bag of tricks and Dr. Phil is no exception. One tactic he uses with patients is role reversal. Using this method, two people trade places to see how each is perceived by the other. So I plan to implement that at my next session. I'll play the therapist and Dr. Phil can be the neurotic.

DEAREST (TV) DIARY

I ALWAYS THOUGHT SOME paunchy, balding, stogey-smoking executive named Nielsen rated TV shows each season. So I was surprised to get a call asking me to complete a viewing diary to help determine the Nielsen Ratings.

"Sure," I said. "What the heck." We don't watch much TV in this house. *Should be a cinch*, I thought.

"How many TVs do you own?" the woman asked.

"Two," I replied. "Unless you count the one that's spent a year by the trash can."

Soon we received two diaries and five crisp dollar bills. I was all set to spend the token of appreciation when the accompanying letter suggested donating it to a good cause instead. Now, I have nothing against charity, but I prefer to make that decision myself, thank you.

I lay the dubious windfall aside and opened one of the diaries. Grabbing a pen, I studied the instructions and completed a lengthy questionnaire. After all that effort, I was reluctant to watch an actual show, knowing I'd have more paperwork to do.

For each program viewed, the survey requested its name, who watched it, time spent, which channel it was on, and the station's call letters. People who leave their set on all day must get carpal tunnel keeping track. There was also a column for indicating whether the TV was on or off at the time. Like maybe we're clairvoyant or something.

I had some questions myself—like how to denote channel surfing. We've been known to spend half an hour clicking the remote and never actually watch a show. Then there are the programs we tune in to for five minutes before shutting them off in disgust.

Furthermore, I'm not sure I want unnamed parties knowing which shows I watch. And while I recall a high school chum recording some pretty tall tales, diaries are *meant* to relate the whole truth, no matter how humiliating.

But the more I thought about the boob tube, the more I wanted to watch a show—*any* show—so I finally gave in. I dutifully jotted down the requested data and then flipped to the comment page in the back.

"Dearest Diary," I wrote, "I'm ashamed to admit this, but I did something utterly deplorable today. Promise you won't tell because I'd be mortified if anyone found out...I watched an entire episode of *Jerry Springer*."

HOME SWEET HOME VIDEO

I FINALLY BOUGHT THE camcorder I bellyached about not having. After saving for eons, it thrilled me to make the transaction and bring home my treasure. And I plan to produce some two-thumbs-up flicks just as soon as I figure it out.

The instructions are in English, but they may as well be Korean like the camera. After wading through an inch-thick manual, I still didn't know how to turn it on.

Now that I've played with it a little, I'm grateful for the "Easy" button, which automatically adjusts settings to no-brainer ones. But I have a few suggestions for the rest of the design.

They might want to rename the operational buttons, for example. Call me picky, but wouldn't it make sense to label the play button "Play" instead of "Light?" Likewise, the stop button could be called something off the wall like "Stop." That way the novice producer may find them when she needs them rather than twenty minutes down the road.

Furthermore, the camera should be made an itty bitty bit bigger so we could use standard sized videotapes. This would eliminate the need for hooking up an unfamiliar camera to an equally foreign VCR. Somehow Dan and I bungled our way through the process without a brawl, but we may not be so lucky in the future.

Rookies like me find it hard to keep the camera steady. As a result, my latest effort includes cameo scenes of the ceiling and floor and action shots of the grass growing. It looks like I was running from the law. But that beats my first attempt when I forgot to remove the lens cap.

Apparently bad home videos are the norm because I ran across an article with tips like these on how to make them more box-office-worthy:

(a) Start with a sign that tells what's coming (i.e., A Boring Home Video).

(b) Don't stand at a distance and zoom in. Move closer, but try not to trip over anything.

(c) Don't forget to tape spectators' reactions (unless they are violent by nature).

(d) Keep each scene brief or your viewers will be Gone With the Wind.

After following these suggestions, I got some noteworthy footage last weekend. Or perhaps I should say "butt"-age, since one subject who shall remain nameless mooned the camera.

I wonder how many thumbs-up that would earn.

IT'S A-BOAT TIME

IT'S A-BOAT TIME summer arrived in these parts. The Happy Yachtsman can finally *use* the high-priced luxury he made payments on the rest of the year.

There's the cost of the vessel itself, unless he opts to tie some logs together. This is followed by registration fees and insurance. Since the motor routinely goes on the fritz, he can chalk up repair bills to the list of expenses. And parking it in the harbor ain't free either.

Or maybe he'll save a few clams by launching it himself. So he rises early and drives down to the harbor where roughly a hundred other avid mariners have communed with *their* boats.

Three hours later it's his turn. Somehow through the grace of God he keeps from launching his truck in the process. But just as he climbs into his cruiser, a squall threatens.

Murphy's Law of Boating dictates that the more expensive his craft, the less spare time he has to actually use it. It looks great sitting in the harbor as he drives by on his way to work. But the one, maybe two, days per month he has to take it out generally call for thunderstorms.

Chances are, he didn't start out with a high-priced craft, but that's another quirk about boats. No matter which size he has, he always yearns for a bigger one. At first his little dinghy brings happiness, but pretty soon he sets his sites on a powerboat. When that grows old, he moves up to a yacht. And before you know it, he can't live without an aircraft carrier.

But whichever vessel he owns, the vision of a calm, peaceful day on the water is still elusive. Just as road rage is on the rise, so is boat rage. Rude cruisers are a given now, cutting other boaters off and causing wakes high enough to surf on. These people would have made great pirates and are just as likely to take a safe boater's course.

.

When the season comes to an end, of course, the Happy Yachtsman needs to winterize his boat. This does not mean abandoning it behind the shed and letting it pile up with snow. It means emptying the gas tank and various other forms of preventative maintenance.

So he can enjoy another carefree boating season next year.

ALL THAT GLITTERS IS NOT GOLDFISH

YOU'D THINK WE'D won the lottery, the way I carried on. But instead the game of chance landed us three goldfish. Unprepared for such a payoff, I ransacked the house for something that could double as a fishbowl. Eventually we broke down and bought a real live aquarium.

We also paid big bucks for a three-inch can of food which, as luck would have it, outlasted the fish. The label warns consumers not to overfeed them. This is as much to prevent a cloudy tank as to thwart a lifelong weight problem.

No expert on *Carassuis Auratus*, I spent awhile researching how to care for them on the Internet. By the time I shut down, Larry had already left this world and Moe was on his last fins. I can't say I grieved for them, though my husband, Dan, was a bit disappointed. I found this ironic since he filleted three bass last week and not a tear was shed.

Larry and Moe's final exit left a large and homely Curly, who wasn't the least bit gold. The lips of his downturned mouth flapped constantly as though he was griping about something, and I entertained myself by lending a voice to his thoughts. Every time I moseyed over to the tank, Curly's little eyeballs focused on me and he stared intently at the stooge on the other side of the glass.

Having recovered from his own near-death experience, Curly seemed of hardier stock than his sidekicks. Not wanting him to be lonely, we went out and bought Larry and Moe the Second.

Generally speaking, most goldfish live about seventy-three hours. This is because pet stores have a seventy-*two* hour return policy. And to get your buck-sixty-nine back, you must bring in the little carcasses, so forget the breading mix.

But get this: some goldfish last up to twenty years. And they can grow as large as a ruler—the twelve-inch variety, I mean, though Napoleon wasn't much bigger. Thus we'd need to trade in our tank for a Jacuzzi.

Unfortunately, Moe the Second and Curly croaked. We suspected foul play and launched a complete investigation. Our findings? Larry Junior is a cold-blooded serial killer—so we won't be bringing him any companions—

Unless we lose another game of chance.

ADDRESSING A STICKY ISSUE

A NONPROFIT ORGANIZATION SENT me some peel-off address labels in today's mail. In return for this generous gift, it asked for a heartfelt donation. In large bills. It even suggested *which* large bills. I was tempted to suggest what it could do with its gift.

As someone who sends her share of letters, I used to like getting "free" address labels. That was years before the other charities jumped on the bandwagon. Since then I have stockpiled them to the point that I could safely mail Texas.

It wouldn't be so bad if they were spelled right, but a fair share of them mutilate my name. And though others get an "A" for their spelling , their print is so small, I have to back into the next town to see it.

This is partly due to their design. I have no beef with big, black letters on a white background, but could happily forgo the folksy clip art. In the faint hope a designer is reading this, I'd like to say, "Quit with the roosters already." And my macho husband, Dan, feels the same about pastel hearts.

Since I'm on a roll, here's another gripe—Why do they call them peel-off when you need a chisel to remove them? I tore through a whole page of them the other day and still came up empty- handed.

For those that *do* come off, Heloise What's-Her-Face offers some practical uses. You can, for example, affix them to the bottoms of casserole dishes to ensure their return. Unless you cook like I do and prefer to remain anonymous.

I wonder what she recommends for surplus greeting cards. Like address labels, they're becoming the choice of more and more charities. Trouble is, they sport this telltale emblem on the back, thus announcing to recipients that I got them free.

Towards the end of the year, another "gift" results in a serious overstock. That's when crowds of calendars arrive with their hands out. In an effort to make themselves useful, they haunt every room but the john.

But the gift most likely to be fruitful and multiply is address labels. This latest pack included a survey, which I dutifully completed. One part read, "I would be interested in receiving the following..." Then it listed cards, labels, calendars and other.

So I checked the last and penned in "a Porsche."

ANSWERING MACHINE RECORDINGS: A PRIMER

"PLEASE LEAVE A MESSAGE," the answering machine said. "We can't answer your call right now because we're in sunny Florida. And you're *not*! Nah-nana-nah-nah!"

"People shouldn't advertise that they're out of town," I griped to my husband, Dan, as I hung up the phone. "They're just asking to be robbed."

"Not many burglars call first," he replied.

He has a point, I suppose. But it's still unwise to broadcast your itinerary to every Bozo who dials your number. It's no one's bees' wax where you are and what you're doing. And most of us don't give a rat's rump.

What matters is that you're not there to talk to. Because if you *were*, you'd pick up the phone, right? You wouldn't...ignore us, would you?

And here's another pet peeve—people who record long, drawn-out messages. ("If this is so-and-so, I'm on my way. If this is Mom, I changed my underwear. If this is an incoming fax, press star-four and your document will self-destruct...") What *is* this—Books on Tape?

Keep it brief (speaking of underwear) and you'll get a lot less hang ups. And record that brief message on a nice short tape so we don't have to wait an hour for the blasted beep.

One of those little instruction books on the market says you should stifle the urge to make a clever recording. I disagree. It could be the only laugh we callers get all day. If you can't think of something entertaining yourself, check out www.answeringmachine.co.uk. For a nominal fee, it offers over three hundred entertaining messages, so you can change it as often as, well, you-know-what.

Throwing in a foreign word or two prompts replies, too—especially from folks dying to show off that they *parlez-vous francais*. Or something to that effect.

Maybe you can do impersonations. Then, go ahead—make my day with one of Clint Eastwood's famous lines. Or stun us with Stallone. But, for the love of Mike, skip Fran Drescher.

Above all, practice your little speech first. Don't wait 'til the tape is rolling to think up something witty. Hire a scriptwriter, if necessary, and rehearse it 'til you get it right. Then maybe—just maybe—I'll leave a message.

And when you get home, you can promptly ignore it.

HOW TO BE A ZILLIONAIRE

ONE OF THE perks of writing a column is that I learn so much from researching it. Take today's topic, for example. After months of doing my homework, I've become somewhat of an expert on stock market terms. And that's no bull.

I used to think, for instance, that stocks were something that controlled criminals. Thanks to Enron and Martha's Mess, I now know it's the other way around.

Growth charts show fluctuating values of stock and look something like a heart monitor screen. For a dead person.

Mutual funds are an investment whereby a number of folks pool their money. Thus they all drown together.

And penny stock is worth even less these days.

I also learned the importance of diversifying, which in lay terms means, "Don't put all your nest eggs in one basket." For example, if your investment portfolio consists of a piggy bank, you should steer some of that wealth into a Christmas Club.

This newfangled focus on finances started when I read a book on how to become filthy stinkin' rich. The advice it set forth included these five common "cents" tips:

(a) Start saving when you're young. (*Now* they tell me.)

(b) Save as much as possible. (A sales clerk told me I could save big bucks on a new computer. Does that count?)

(c) Earn compound interest. (Making interest on my interest? Hmmm...interesting.)

(d) Leave your money in the account 'til the cows come home. (If not longer.)

(e) Choose something that pays a high rate of interest. (That would exclude my savings account. If its rates drop any lower, I'll have to pay the bank.)

So I looked into bonds and discovered there are various types. You've got your Patriot Bond, your H Bond, and your James Bond. R-R. As I understand it, no one recalls what the "EE" in "EE Bonds" stood for so they changed the name to Patriot Bonds. These can be purchased for as little as twenty-five bucks—the cost of a night on the town, less the hangover.

At press time, they paid nearly four times the interest of my sorry savings account. Best of all, they're risk-free. As someone who walks a mile to avoid ladders, that suits me just fine.

But despite all my research, it took my hairdresser to ultimately convince me. She said that bonds have more fun.

WAXING ON ABOUT SALON SERVICES

I USED TO GO to beauty shops for a haircut, a dye job and the latest poop from the grapevine. But now they offer an even wider variety of services. If one has money to burn, there are a number of novel ways to ignite it at your local salon.

Speaking of fire, ear candling tops the list of new developments. Patrons who participate in this service lie on their side and a hollow candle is placed in their ear. (In case you try this at home, the flame end points *away* from the head.) Twins receiving the treatment look like a matching set of candle holders.

At any rate, according to the ads, the ear becomes cleansed as unsightly residue is drawn into the candle's opening. Personally, I'd be reluctant to share that with my hairdresser, no matter how well we were acquainted. I can just hear the conversation when I'm out of earshot. "Man, you should've seen the dregs that came out!"

Still, those who have tried it find it very therapeutic. Furthermore, many report auditory improvement, hearing gossip far better after a session. But I've waxed on about that long enough. It's time to move on to the next service, which is...

...acrylic nails. Any beauty shop worth its scissors claims a resident nail technician, who offers manicures and pedicures. And chances are, you've seen ladies around town sporting unbelievably long claws, thanks to acrylic nails. This popular procedure involves applying a mixture of polymer powder and a fast drying liquid, which is then shaped, filed and buffed into strong, beautiful talons. I'd try it myself, but have a hard time getting my socks on as it is.

Another service many salons offer is massage therapy. For those with their minds in the sewer, the kneading, rhythmic motions of a Swedish massage are strictly for stress relief. I've seen this done in movies and felt my shoulders limber up just watching it. As effective as valium, this could be every bit as habit forming.

And they have other means of rubbing folks the right way. Most of the therapeutic massages contain at least twelve letters, with the exception of one. The mud wrap involves applying oil and clay and then sealing the body with a cellophane-like substance. It's perfectly suited to those with an "earthy" personality like mine.

But I think I'll have to pass.

GONNA DIET NOW

I HEAR THE THEME song from the movie *Rocky* fairly often. "Gonna Fly Now" pops into my head each time I start a diet-and-exercise program—something I do with nauseating frequency. The tune inspired Rocky to shape up for three entire minutes and has the same effect on me.

Perhaps inspiration would last longer if I found a diet I could live with. Despite an interesting array on the market, I have yet to find one that fits my lifestyle. For example, you've no doubt heard of...

...the Food Combining Diet. As its name implies, it recommends eating vittles in certain combinations—high protein with non-starch, etc. Trouble is, it nixes my favorite mixes. Fries and a shake...cake and ice cream...that sort of thing.

Then there's the Blood Type Diet. Based on Dr. Peter D'Adamo's book, *Eat Right 4 Your Type*, it introduces the idea that one should eat certain foods based on one's plasma. As and ABs function best on grains and carbohydrates. Os thrive on red meat, but Bs should "steer" clear of it. Until I recall my blood type, however, this diet is not 4 me.

Another dilly is the Russian Air Force Diet. They should rename it the Meat and Coffee Diet as it places heavy emphasis on these, much to my vegetarian taste buds' dismay. Speaking of rushin' air forces, I find the Cabbage Soup Diet a bit more palatable, though I'm less likely to keep dinner guests.

While the All You Can Eat* Diet sounds tempting, it turns out you can only choose from one boring food group per day. As a result, they should expand the title to add *Without Gagging.

Another option is the Pasta-Chocolate Diet. Granted, it features my two favorite foods, but only one ounce of chocolate is allowed. Now who could leave half a candy bar? And though I like the concept that linguini and fettucini can help me wear a bikini, there's a catch— no rich, fattening sauces allowed. Are they off their noodle?

Which brings me to my favorite—the Subway Diet, so called because its creator was once the size of a train. But when Jared Fogle started chew-chewing two low-fat sub sandwiches per day, he lost two-hundred-forty-five pounds. Honest engine.

So I think I'm "gonna fly" with *his* diet. And hope I'm not grounded.

BETTING AWAY FROM IT ALL

A RASH OF BANK robberies over the past year has been attributed to gambling debts. I'm surprised there've been no *casino* robberies to pay off bank debts. They seem to have more of the big bucks.

A commercial for a local casino convinced me that my hubby and I should pay it a visit (key word being "pay"). The people on the ad seemed the picture of happiness, so naturally I expected that scenario. But the patrons I met looked bored silly even as coins tumbled out of their slot machines.

"You won! You won!" I gushed to one lady, who explained to this neophyte that it was *her* money to start with.

Another woman was downright grumpy. With a scowl on her face, she watched me play a nickel at a time. "You're not gonna get anything that way," she said in disgust. "If you wanna win, you've gotta put in three or four at once." After dispensing this advice, she wandered away. Empty handed.

Whatever happened to one-arm bandits? Like everything else, slot machines are computerized now. You merely push a button to set the apples and oranges in motion. I liked it better when they were mechanical. It felt like I had some control over my fruitiness.

For those who don't *mind* leaving their financial fate in electronic hands, they can bet away from it all at home. Online gambling sites offer everything from bingo to roulette. As fast-paced as the real McCoy, you can file for Chapter 11 in no time.

I'm too miserly to go that route, but I do buy instant lottery tickets on occasion. Trouble is, there are too many to choose from. "Pick a card...any card," the cashier says as she fans them out. Then the customers behind me sigh in unison as I eenie-meenie-minie-moe it.

New cards are constantly introduced and just when I have the instructions figured out, they change them. "Match your numbers to *this*, win *that*! Match your numbers to *that*, win *this*! No match? You *lose*, buddy!" With my lucky key, I scratch the card furiously and study it for an hour before realizing I lost.

Then I read the fine print on the back. "If you bet more than you can afford to lose, you've got a problem."

I'd wager they're right about that.

.

THE LIGHTER SIDE OF LYRICS

INABILITY TO HOLD a tune has never stopped me from singing. I even belonged to a choir 'til they found out who was making the racket.

Though I warble all kinds of music, my favorites are Golden Oldies no matter how mystifying they may be. Remember the Guess Who and its hit, "No Time"? I could never figure out what they meant by, "No time for the killing floors." Should linoleum appear on a public offender list?

Then there was Neil Diamond's, "I am I said." He belted that out as though it made perfect sense, didn't he? The Beatles expanded on the subject with, "I am he as you are he as you are me and we are all together." Is that concept a bit fuzzy or is it just me? (Or he? Or we?)

One thing *is* clear, though. Plenty of songs ring with bad grammar. In "Small Town," John Cougar sang, "No, I cannot forget from where it is that I come from." My guess is he didn't come from English class.

But whether they make sense or not, I tickle my vocal chords with reckless abandon. Trouble is, most songs were written by men. Catchy tunes or not, I feel *really* awkward singing songs like, "I Wanna Kiss the Bride." Songs with girls' names don't sit well with me either. I always know when my fetching neighbor strolls by—my Better Half breaks out with, "Hey, Hey Paula!"

When it comes to comical song titles, country music wins hand-organs down. If I knew the melodies, I'd have fun jamming to tunes like, "How Can I Miss You if You Won't Go Away?" Or "I'd Rather

Pass a Kidney Stone than Another Night with You." Or my personal favorite, "I Still Miss You, Baby, but My Aim is Getting Better."

Though I rarely forget a tune, my memory often malfunctions when it comes to lyrics. I routinely have to fake them at some point in every song. Anyone listening knows I'm close but no sitar.

That's why I like singing in church, where the right words are as near as my hymnal. I have to keep changing octaves, though, as the low notes are too low and the high notes, too high. If I tried to reach them, I'd shatter the stained glass windows.

And end up cryin' in the chapel.

CAPTURING THOSE PHOTO (FL)OPS...

THERE'S A CAMERA OUT now that's so small you can swallow it whole. Designed to photograph a person's innards, it shares a one-inch capsule with a battery, radio transmitter and light. The picture featured in the article I read clearly depicted someone's small intestine. Imagine using that for a Christmas card—Happy Holidays from Corky's Colon!

What a contrast to the *camera obscura*, contrived in the 1300s by a dude named Roger Bacon. Rather than it going inside of people, people went inside of *it*. In the trivia department, *obscura* is Latin for dark room, and it was basically an empty shed with a lens in each side. When light filtered through, an image appeared upside down on the opposite wall. This could then be printed out and ironed on a T-shirt.

Along came George Eastman five-hundred-odd-years later and invented the first unobscure camera. It was one of those big box doohickeys with black fabric attached to the back. To take a picture the photographer ducked his head under the cloth, thus looking like me when I exit the shower.

Since then, cameras have steadily shrunk. One of today's cameras can fit onto a cell phone, allowing people to take snapshots and transmit them to other cell phones. That way they can photograph the scene of the accident they caused by gabbing instead of watching the road.

Less obvious is the tiny digital spy camera. It takes pictures by remote control so people are unaware they're being photographed. I "shutter" to think what it could be used for.

Camcorders have gone on a diet, too. The one I used to lug around left a permanent crater on my right shoulder. But the Otago

Polytechnic School of Information Technology came up with a device that won't cause injuries—though it may record them. The tiny ball-cam was designed to fit inside sports equipment to transmit a ball's eye-view of the action.

I'm more interested in a gadget I saw on Oprah's show. The size of a credit card and every bit as expensive, it functions as either a digital camera or a camcorder. 'Til now I've hauled both to special events. And my 35-millimeter, for good measure. But I'd gladly give all of that up for Oprah's pick.

What better way to capture the next photo (fl)op?

THE QUEEN OF CLEAN

I WELCOMED THE SUNBEAM streaming through my window as I chatted with a friend. Little did I realize it illuminated a cobweb the size of Mount Fuji. Normally I wouldn't give a flip, but this pal of mine is the Queen of Clean. In fact, she housekeeps for a living. Knowing my shortcomings in the French Maid department, this in itself is ironic.

Thelma is one of those Heloise-type people who know a-hundred-and-one uses for baking soda. You name the spot and she can get it out. Why, she could clean a dirty joke. Disinfect it, too.

I have, on occasion, paid her visits in the hope of finding a smidgeon of grime or a wayward crumb or two. But much to my disappointment, the woman shows not the slightest hint of slovenliness. Don't get me wrong. I don't actually go looking for other people's dirt, but it tends to jump out at me in a foreign environment. It's when I'm home that I'm oblivious to it.

Oh, sure, I get a hankering to clean things up once in a while, but that usually ends in disaster. Like the time the vacuum swallowed something that disagreed with it and threw up on my rug. Or when I tried removing a tiny stain and smeared it into a three-inch blob.

I try not to take advantage of Thelma's expertise, but times like that call for professional advice. So I consult her for some pro bono (also known as free) counsel.

"Got any Ajax?" she'll reply, and before I know it, my cleaning dilemma is solved.

If Thelma has one quirk, it's that she can't sit for long. She doesn't need 20-Mule Team—she *is* a 20-Mule Team. It's a given that

at some point during visits, she will wander off and disappear for
awhile. No need to call 9-1-1 though—she's just working out a stain.

All of this makes me somewhat paranoid about entertaining her.
But if she notices the layer of cat hair clinging to the couch, she never
mentions it. She doesn't have to. Like the telltale heart, I give myself
away.

"Er...let's sit somewhere else," I say as I lead her away. "Like
your house."

A FRIENDLY BREED

MAYBE IT'S JUST a "girl" thing, but I have yet to see my hubby send
someone a thinking-of-you card. Dan is far more inclined to call a
crony with something meaningful like, "How the heck are ya?"

He doesn't get wrapped up in his friends' personal problems
either. I, on the other hand, assume not only my own, but those of
everyone in my address book.

But, male or female, we've encountered similar types of
acquaintances over the years. For example:

You've heard of user friendly? Well, some chums are *friendly
users*. "Hey, pal! How's it goin'? Can I use your pruning shears?" Or
"Say, can I borrow your car?" In fact, that's the *only* time they come
around. Friends in need are a friendly breed.

There's no shortage of *advice-giving friends* either. I was one
myself 'til I learned how irritating they are. When someone unloads,
you feel compelled to respond with something constructive, but people
don't *want* advice. They want loyal, compassionate comrades who will
shut up and listen.

Then there are *"honest" friends*. These folks seize every
opportunity to be brutally frank. True quote from a former (key word)
friend of mine: "This dress'll fit you—it's *huge*!" The epitaph
following her murder will likely read, "She said it for their own good."

My best chum was a *gradual friend*—one I knew for years before
we started hanging out. At the opposite end of the spectrum are *hit-
and-run friends*, to quote a new (and hopefully lasting) cohort. This
happens when you instantly bond with certain people, only to have
them vanish from your life without a trace. Similarly, *now-you-see-'em
friends* disappear without notice, but re-emerge when they tire of their
other pals.

Dan and I have seen our share of *"three-in-one" friends*, too. They give you the lowdown on "me, myself and I," but rarely ask about *us*. We'd much rather spend an afternoon reminiscing with *old friends*. Trouble is, we never do anything *new* to reminisce about.

In our ninety-two combined years, we've learned three important things about friendships:

(a) Age doesn't matter—and the older we get, the more this applies.

(b) Keep an open mind. People you least expect can be durn good buddies.

(c) Never exceed your tolerance level. That may mean getting together on a weekly or monthly basis.

Or every other decade.

DON'T ASK, DON'T TELL

IT WAS MORE of a rhetorical question. When I asked, "Hey, how are ya?" I meant it as a polite greeting.

But he took me literally and held me hostage in the grocery store for twenty-odd minutes. The subject of his monologue, as I lapsed in and out of consciousness, concerned his recent surgery, which he described in mind-numbing detail. After emerging from my coma, I resumed shopping only to find him cornering someone in another aisle.

People are funny when it comes to their ailments. Rare is the patient who keeps his medical problems to himself. And because it happened to him or her, the symptoms are far worse than what anyone else would suffer. ("Honey, you don't know pain 'til you've passed a gallstone.")

Whether it be heart bypass surgery or the heartbreak of psoriasis, they feel a deep need to share the experience with friends, associates and even total strangers. And for many, the bigger the audience, the better.

When a chum and I dined out a while back, our waitress took advantage of the caucus to relay her adventure in stomach stapling. Her lecture set forth pre-surgery measures, the operation itself and her ongoing recovery. I don't know about *her* appetite, but my pal and I lost all interest in food.

A former co-worker of mine preferred to share her ailments with people one at a time. So she'd haunt one department after another 'til she enlightened them all or suffered her next malady, whichever came first. She could have saved the company big bucks by circulating a memo.

That, of course, would invite typos. I'm reminded of the one I saw concerning SARS which listed, as one of its telltale symptoms, a "whopping" cough...

At any rate, this same gal had a tendency to toss out hints like, "I hope I'm not coming down with something." As a result, no one was too shocked when she'd call in sick the next day. Or when she returned to relay the ordeal.

It might not be so bad if people kept the more intimate details to themselves, but they seem to thrive on the nitty-gritty.

Or if they asked how *I'm* doing for a change. Then I could tell them about this whopping cough I've got...

SHE SHOOTS! SHE BORES!

NORMALLY I SIDESTEP OUR newspaper's sports section. Not what you'd call an active person, I can't relate to articles based solely on motion.

But to research this column I scanned months' worth of headlines from my personal archives. It became clear to me that violence pervades today's sports. Teams aren't just beaten these days. They're belted, throttled, trounced on, pounded, and in *some* cases, even slain.

I get a kick out of their tough-sounding names, though—Lions and Tigers and Bears, oh my! Strangely enough, team names often determine their headline fate. The Panthers tend to "maul" their opponents as often as the Jets "soar." How clever.

Photos for these games attest to their brutality. Regardless of the sport, most athletes wear a grimace, as though forced to sample my Tuna Surprise. Two wrestlers in particular looked like they dined at Corky's Cafe. At least I *think* there were two. It's hard counting when they're tangled up like that.

I also saw a disgruntled coach with a headset. From his facial expression, I'd guess he wasn't jammin' to the oldies.

I'm impressed with our local sport photographer's work, though. His sharp, in-your-face photos bring heart-pounding reality to high school write-ups. And he does this with a minimum of armpit shots.

The stories, too, are fraught with realism. It takes a special person to write highly detailed accounts like that. I could watch a two-hour game and still not have the presence of mind to relay a single highlight. There are two reasons for this:

(a) I'm not what you'd call observant. The lady you honked at last week when the light turned green? Yours truly.

(b) Every sport has its peculiar jargon for which I need a translator. So I bought this book called *The Complete Sports Dictionary*, George Sullivan, author, which defines words pertaining to every contest imaginable.

"Bed," for example, refers to the flat surface on a pool table. One must "draw" a bow in archery. A "split" is something you don't want to see while bowling. "Sheets" are ropes used to adjust sails. And "stealing" is perfectly legal in baseball.

All of which remind me of my *favorite* sport—"stealing" off to "bed" and "drawing" up the "sheets."

And on that note, I'll make like an ax and "split."

Lois A. Corcoran

Lois Corcoran's humor column appears in newspapers in the Great Lakes area. She lives in Michigan's beautiful Upper Peninsula and welcomes email at corky@dsnet.us. Download her latest book, "The Dine All Day Diet" from http://www.dppstore.com.

Printed in the United States
68391LVS00001B/49-54

9 780759 947825